THE CHECKLIST SERIES

MANAGING OTHERS

TEAMS AND INDIVIDUALS

Chartered
Management
Institute

PROFILE BOOKS

First published in Great Britain in 2013 by
Profile Books Ltd
3a Exmouth House
Pine Street
Exmouth Market
London EC1R 0JH
www.profilebooks.com

10 9 8 7 6 5 4 3 2 1

A CIP catalogue record for this book is available from the British Library.

ISBN: 978 1 78125 144 7
eISBN: 978 1 84765 975 0

Text design by sue@lambledesign.demon.co.uk

Typeset in Helvetica by MacGuru Ltd
info@macguru.org.uk

Printed and bound in Britain by Bell & Bain Ltd

The table on page 10 was previously published in *Team Roles at Work* by R. Meredith Belbin (Butterworth Heinemann, 2010) and is reproduced by kind permission of Taylor & Francis Books (UK).

The diagram on page 97 was previously published in *Motivation and Personality* by Abraham H. Maslow, Robert D. Frager and James Fadiman, 3rd edition, © 1987. Adapted by permission of Pearson Education, Inc., Upper Saddle River, NJ.

The diagram on page 100 was previously published in *How to Motivate People: A Guide for Managers* by Twyla Dell (Kogan Page, 1989, page 27).

The diagram on page 164 was previously published in *The Manual of Learning Styles* © 1996 Peter Honey and Alan Mumford, published by Pearson TalentLens, a division of Pearson Education Ltd. Reproduced by permission. All rights reserved.

All reasonable efforts have been made to obtain permission to reproduce copyright material. Any omissions or errors of attribution are unintentional and will be corrected in future printings following notification in writing to the publisher.

MIX
Paper from
responsible sources
FSC® C007785

About the checklist series

Management can be a daunting task. Managers are expected to provide direction, foster commitment, facilitate change and achieve results through the efficient, creative and responsible deployment of people and other resources. On top of that, managers have to manage themselves and develop their own personal skills. Just keeping up is a challenge – and we cannot be experts in everything.

The checklists in this series have been developed over many years by the Chartered Management Institute (CMI) to meet this challenge by addressing the main issues that managers can expect to face during their career. Each checklist distils good practice from industry to provide a clear and straightforward overview of a specific topic or activity, and has been reviewed by CMI's Subject Matter Experts Panel to reflect new research and changes in working life.

The series is designed both for managers who need an introduction to unfamiliar topics, and for those who want to refresh their understanding of the salient points. In more specialised areas – for example, financial management – checklists can also enable the generalist manager to work more effectively with experts, or to delegate more effectively to a subordinate.

Why is the checklist format useful? Checklists provide a logical, structured framework to help professional managers deal with an increasingly complex workplace – they help shape our thoughts and save us from being confused by too much information. At the same time, checklists help us to make good use of what we already know. They help us to remember things and prevent us from forgetting something important. Thus, no matter how expert we may already be, using checklists can improve outcomes and give us the confidence to manage more effectively, and to get the job done.

About this book

Managing Others – Teams and Individuals is aimed at anyone who manages a team, whether large or small. Using a combination of action-oriented checklists and handy short summaries of the ideas of seminal management thinkers on individual motivation and team behaviour, it will guide you through the basics of selecting and building a successful team. It will then help you motivate and develop individuals to enable your team to achieve a consistently high standard. As well as introducing you to valuable skills such as coaching and mentoring, this concise and indispensable handbook will also equip you for difficult situations such as managing conflict, dealing with bullying and breaking bad news to help you become an effective and capable manager.

Contents

Coaching and mentoring

Managing difficult situations

Introduction

It is now over forty years since I first became a manager, but I can still remember the trepidation with which I faced the new challenges of the role in those first days. Like many, if not most, new managers, I had moved straight from a technical position and had to learn fast.

There are of course technical aspects of management, but above all management is about people and making the transition from doing a good job oneself to getting the best out of other people. While we all need to develop a management style appropriate to our own personality, there are many well-tried approaches to use.

That is what this book addresses in a series of comprehensive checklists that cover, in practical and helpful detail, most of the ways in which a manager is likely to interact with others, both below and above him or her in an organisation. Each checklist starts with a description of a typical situation (team briefing, for example), followed by a detailed list of action points and a reminder of key things to avoid.

Usefully interspersed among these checklists are short profiles of some of the great management gurus, from Herzberg and Maslow to Adair and Bennis. While describing their theories, these sections also comment on ways in which others have developed or challenged their views – an important reminder that the changing structure of organisations (for example the flatter structures made possible by modern technology) may well require the original approach to be modified.

At a time when we have to look to business to pull us out of recession, we need all our managers to be as effective as possible right from the start of their managerial careers. This book, together with the rest of the CMI checklist series, is an invaluable aid in that objective, while also providing useful advice on how to handle specific situations that may occur less often, such as how to deal with 'plateaued performers' for example. Bullying is covered too – importantly, because CMI research suggests that sadly this is still all too common in the workplace.

This practical guide is well designed and easy to use. I thoroughly recommend it.

Sir Anthony Cleaver
Chairman, Novia Financial plc

Steps in successful team building

A team is more than just a group of people who happen to work together. It is a group of people working towards common goals and objectives and sharing responsibility for the outcomes. Team building is the process of selecting and grouping team members effectively, and developing good working relationships and practices that enable the team to steer and develop the work and reach their goals. Increasingly, a team may be composed of people drawn from different functions, departments and disciplines who have been brought together for a specific project.

The use of workplace teams to carry out projects of various kinds has become widespread. Teams can play a key role in organisational success, but the development of good working relationships is crucial to team performance. Organisations that take the time and trouble to invest in the development of positive interaction and cooperation in teams will reap the benefits of improved morale, more effective performance and the successful completion of projects.

Successful team building can:

- coordinate the efforts of individuals as they tackle complex tasks
- make the most of the expertise and knowledge of all those involved, which might otherwise remain untapped
- raise and sustain motivation and confidence as individual team members feel supported and involved

- encourage members to bounce ideas off each other, solve problems and find appropriate ways forward
- help break down communication barriers and avoid unhealthy competition, rivalry and point-scoring across departments
- raise the level of individual and collective empowerment
- enhance engagement with and ownership of the task in hand.

This checklist provides an outline of the main steps in the development of workplace teams, but does not cover aspects specific to virtual or remote teams.

Action checklist

1 Consider whether you really do need a team

Don't assume that a team is necessarily the best way of achieving the objectives you have in mind. Think carefully about the tasks that need to be completed and the skills required before forming a team. Teamwork may not always be the best approach – it may be difficult, for example, in an organisation with a culture of rigid reporting structures or fixed work procedures. Ask yourself whether one person with the relevant knowledge and skills could carry out the task more effectively.

It is also important to weigh the advantages and disadvantages of teamworking – there may be losses in coordination and motivation if teams are not carefully developed and managed. Consider whether there is a need for a mix of skills and experience, the sharing of workloads, or brainstorming and problem solving. In such cases a team will often be the best option.

2 Define objectives and the skills needed to reach them

Think carefully about the nature of the tasks or projects to be carried out by the team and the mix of knowledge and skills needed. For teams handling routine tasks on a long-term basis, low levels of diversity in the team and clear definitions of tasks and roles are required. In this context, the main aims would be high levels of team cohesion and commitment and low levels of conflict.

For innovation and problem solving, however, high levels of diversity and complementary skills will be required and the definition of goals and roles may be left to the team. This might involve losses in coordination, much less cohesion and fairly high potential for conflict, but could be worthwhile if new ideas and solutions are required.

3 Take team roles into account

The work of R. Meredith Belbin provides some useful insights into the patterns of behaviour exhibited by team members and the way they interact with each other. You may wish to take these into account when putting a team together or seeking to shape an existing team. Belbin identifies a number of roles which team members can play and their respective strengths and weaknesses. He suggests that teams need a balance of members with differing roles if they are to work together effectively. Furthermore, an understanding of personal differences and roles can help team members to cooperate more successfully, complementing each other's strengths.

4 Plan a team-building strategy

Invest time at the outset in getting the operating framework right so that the team will develop and grow.

The following aspects should be considered:

- **a climate of trust** – where mistakes and failures are viewed as learning experiences, not occasions to apportion blame
- **the free flow of information** – to enable team members to integrate their work with business objectives
- **training** – in interpersonal skills, including communication and negotiation. Training may also be needed in handling the tasks required and taking responsibility for them. Team leaders will

need project management skills and the ability to manage meetings and moderate discussions

- **time** – ensure that the team has the time needed to coordinate activities, develop thoughts and ideas, monitor progress and hold regular meetings, and has access to the resources needed to achieve its objectives

- **resources** – make sure that the team has access to any resources and materials it needs to complete the work

- **objectives** – these need to be clearly understood by all team members. This is increasingly a matter of involving team members in setting objectives rather than dictating prescribed objectives to them

- **tasks and roles** – team members must be absolutely clear about what is expected of them and what tasks have to be carried out

- **feedback** – everybody needs to know how well they are doing and if and where improvements can be made. Feedback should focus primarily on the positive aspects and on ways of addressing any problems or difficulties.

5 Get the team together

At the initial meeting you should aim to start building the team as a team rather than a collection of individuals. Discuss and agree the outcomes the team is to achieve, rather than attempting to address the detailed issues involved in the project or task. Bear in mind that most teams pass through several stages of growth before starting to produce their best work. Bruce Tuckman's 1965 model of team development presents this process in the following stages:

- forming – as team members come together

- storming – as they work through the issues

- norming – as conflicts are resolved and working practices and expectations are established

- performing – as objectives are achieved.

Bear in mind that these stages vary in importance depending on the type of task being carried out. For example, in the case of routine tasks, groups should proceed more quickly to performing. Teams with innovative tasks will need more time for forming and storming and often never reach the performing stage. Once a problem-solving strategy has been found by an 'innovative' team, it may be necessary to form a new team to implement the solution.

Make sure that everyone knows what their personal contribution to the team's success will be, its place in the project schedule and its importance to the project's success.

6 Explore and establish operating ground rules

Agree processes for decision-making and reporting for the life span of the team. Establish when and how often meetings will take place and how they will be managed. Encourage a climate of open and honest communication, so that, as far as possible, team members will be able to express opinions without fear of recrimination and minority views will be heard and considered.

7 Identify individuals' strengths

Carry out an audit of individuals' strengths and place people in the right position based on their skills and competences. Consider also how contributions and responsibilities overlap and how synergy can be released. It is important for team members to reach a common understanding of each other's strengths, so that they can work together efficiently. This will help to integrate the skills of team members, strengthen team cohesion and improve the performance of the team as a whole.

You may also consider bringing in someone with team-building experience to help with the initial phases, especially if the team's task is major or complex.

8 See yourself as a team member

Your role as team leader is to be a member of the team, not just the boss. Make it clear that everyone in the team has an important role to play and that your role happens to be that of team leader. Act as a role model and maintain effective communication with all members, especially through listening. Be aware of the formal and informal roles within the team and endeavour to keep conflict between them to a minimum. In some cases it may be beneficial for roles to remain fluid, adding to the flexibility of working relationships, but don't allow team members to lose their focus on their individual strengths or objectives. An effective leader may decide to cede project leadership, albeit temporarily, to another when specific skills are required.

9 Check progress towards objectives

Check regularly to ensure that everyone still has a clear focus on what they are working towards, both individually and as a team. Identify milestones and hold team members accountable for progress towards them. As the team develops pride in shared success and lessons learned from failure, this should help to develop a sense of shared purpose, strengthen commitment and contribute to improved performance in the long run.

10 Time meetings with care

Unnecessary meetings are a bane, but if there are too few, the project – and the team – can lose focus. Meet regularly but with purpose:

- to provide an opportunity to check 'how are we doing?'
- to review progress on the task
- to reflect on how the team is working.

If any problems are identified, plan and implement appropriate action or corrective measures.

11 Dissolve the team

When the team has accomplished its tasks, acknowledge this. Carry out a final review to see if objectives have been achieved and evaluate the team's performance, so that team members may learn, improve and benefit from experience. If all the objectives have been met, the team can be disbanded.

As a manager you should avoid:

- expecting a new team to perform effectively from the word go
- dominating the work of the team, whether intentionally, unintentionally or even unconsciously
- exercising excessive control which may stifle creativity
- overlooking the impact of formal and informal team roles
- allowing the team to lose focus on the tasks to be completed
- letting a team become too exclusive, in case it loses touch with the rest of the organisation
- allowing individuals to take credit for the achievements of the team.

R. Meredith Belbin
Team building

Introduction

R. Meredith Belbin (b. 1926) is acknowledged as the father of team role theory. As a result of research carried out in the 1970s, he identified eight (later extended to nine) useful roles which are necessary for a successful team. His contribution has gained in significance because of the widespread adoption of teamworking in the late 1980s and 1990s.

Belbin is an academic who has also spent periods working in industry and who now has his own consultancy company. It was while working at the Industrial Training Research Unit in Cambridge in the UK that he was asked by Henley Management College to conduct some research into the operation of management teams.

The college's approach to management education was based on group work, and it had been noticed that some teams of individually able executives performed poorly and others well. This impression was reinforced when a business game was introduced to one of the courses. Belbin discovered that it was the contribution of particular personality types rather than the merits of individuals that were important to the success and failure of such teams.

There has been a continuing interest in Belbin's work because teamworking is increasingly an important strategy for organisations. There are many reasons for this. Teamworking is variously seen as a means of:

- providing greater worker flexibility and cooperation
- helping to achieve cultural shifts within an organisation
- improving problem solving and project management
- tapping the talents of everyone in the organisation.

There are different types of teamworking: for example, temporary teams, cross-functional teams, top management teams and self-directed teams.

This interest in teams means that team building, including team selection, group dynamics and team performance, has become particularly important. Although there are many models of team relationships, such as Team Management Systems (TMS) developed by Charles Margerison and Dick McCann, Belbin's model is probably the best known.

Team role theory

It is important to remember that Belbin's findings relate to teams of managers rather than other types of team. They were first published in *Management Teams: Why They Succeed or Fail* and later refined in *Team Roles at Work*.

Belbin says that a team role 'describes a pattern of behaviour characteristic of the way in which one team member interacts with another where his performance serves to facilitate the progress of the team as a whole'.

The essence of his theory is that, given knowledge of the abilities and characteristics of individual team members, success or failure can be predicted within certain limits. As a result, unsuccessful teams can be improved through analysis of their shortcomings and making changes. But it is also important for individuals within the team to understand the roles that others play, when and how to let another team member take over, and how to compensate for shortcomings.

Although each of the nine roles has to be filled for a team to work

	Roles and descriptions team-role contribution	Allowable weaknesses
PL	**Plant** Creative, imaginative, unorthodox. Solves difficult problems.	Ignores incidentals. Too preoccupied to communicate effectively.
RI	**Resource investigator** Extrovert enthusiastic, communicative. Explores opportunities. Develops contacts.	Over-optimistic. Loses interest once initial enthusiasm has passed.
CO	**Co-ordinator** Mature, confident, a good chairperson. Clarifies goals, promotes decision-making, delegates well.	Can often be seen as manipulative. Offloads personal work.
SH	**Shaper** Challenging, dynamic, thrives on pressure. The drive and courage to overcome obstacles.	Prone to provocation. Offends people's feelings.
ME	**Monitor evaluator** Sober, strategic and discerning. Sees all options. Judges accurately.	Lacks drive and ability to inspire others.
TW	**Team worker** Co-operative, mild, perceptive and diplomatic. Listens, builds, averts friction.	Indecisive in crunch situations.
IMP	**Implementer** Disciplined, reliable, conservative and efficient. Turns ideas into practical actions.	Somewhat inflexible. Slow to respond to new possibilities.
CF	**Completer-finisher** Painstaking, conscientious, anxious. Searches out errors and omissions. Delivers on time.	Inclined to worry unduly. Reluctant to delegate.
SP	**Specialist** Single-minded, self-starting, dedicated. Provides knowledge and skills in rare supply.	Contributes only on a narrow front. Dwells on technicalities.

Figure 1: Team roles – contributions and allowable weaknesses

effectively, they are not needed in equal measure, nor are they needed at the same time. There can be fewer than nine people in a team, since people are capable of taking on back-up roles where there is less need for them to fulfil a primary team role.

These roles are determined largely by the psychological make-up of those who instinctively adopt them, measured in terms of four principal factors: intelligence; dominance; extroversion/introversion; and stability/anxiety. The ratings are shown as traits in the list of team role contributions.

The self-perception inventory and the Interplace system

Belbin devised a self-perception inventory, which has been through several revisions, as a quick and easy way for individual managers to work out what their own team roles should be. It was, however, taken up by organisations and used to determine employees' team types, and it has been questioned whether it is psychometrically acceptable for this purpose. Academics were concerned that it was too subjective and recommended that feedback should come instead from a range of sources. In response to this criticism, Belbin reiterated that the inventory was not designed for this purpose and developed a computerised system called Interplace to cater for the needs of organisations.

Interplace is a more sophisticated approach to role analysis than the self-perception inventory because it incorporates feedback from other people, not just the individual concerned. The main inputs to the Interplace system are data from self-perception exercises, observer assignments and job-requirement evaluations. Interplace filters, scores, stores, converts and interprets the data gathered. It offers advice based on the three inputs in terms of counselling, team role chemistry, career development, and behaviours needed in certain jobs and team positions. The system works as a diagnostic and development tool for organisations.

Later theories

In the 1990s, Belbin extended his work by exploring the link between teams and the organisational environment in which they operate. He suggests that an effective model for the new flatter organisation may be a spiral or helix in which individuals and teams move forward on the basis of excellence rather than function.

Belbin has also devised a system for defining jobs that he calls 'Workset'. The aim is to define the boundaries and content of a job through interactive communication between the manager and the job-holder. Colour is used to denote different aspects of the job. There should be five main outcomes:

- the facilitation of empowerment
- the encouragement of greater job flexibility
- the promotion of teamworking
- the support of cultural change
- a continuous improvement process for jobs and job-holders

It is too early to say what impact the progression helix theory or Workset system will have. They are undoubtedly a contribution, however, to managing in today's de-layered organisations and flexible working environments, with the associated need to involve and communicate with staff.

In perspective

Although independent recent research has thrown doubt on the existence of nine separate team roles, Belbin's broad findings have not been questioned, nor has the popularity of his theories been disputed. There has been an enduring interest in team role categories on the part of managers in a wide variety of organisations. This is because:

- there is an increasing interest in teamworking
- Belbin made his ideas accessible to the lay person
- Belbin is recognised as the first to develop our understanding of the dynamics of teams.

Get the right people and get the people right

'Getting the right people' means planning and carrying out the recruitment process so as to secure people whose knowledge, skills and observable behaviours are consistent with the needs of the business and can add significant value in the job to which they are appointed.

'Getting the people right' means adopting policies and practices for the induction, training and development of new employees that are fair and consistent in design and application. It also entails integrating them into the organisation and involving them as partners in the business. This depends on recognising that the employment relationship is an ongoing process in which the manager seeks to secure the fullest voluntary contribution of each individual, corresponding to the value that the organisation invests in the employee.

Managing people is perhaps the most challenging and – if you get it right – rewarding of all management activities. Good people management plays a key role in:

- developing good working relationships
- creating a positive organisational culture
- boosting morale and job satisfaction
- engaging employees
- enhancing performance
- unlocking employee potential.

Line managers at all levels in the organisation – from senior managers responsible for setting HR policy and strategy to frontline managers responsible for managing the employment relationship on a day-to-day basis – play a crucial role in managing and engaging employees, as has been highlighted by recent research carried out by the Chartered Management Institute and Penna, a global HR services organisation. Personnel specialists work with line managers to ensure that HR policies reflect good practice and provide information and advice to maintain quality standards. In larger organisations, transactional personnel activities are carried out by the HR function; in smaller organisations without an HR specialist, managers may carry out these activities. This checklist provides an introduction to the main people management responsibilities for those new to the role.

Action checklist

1   Plan the recruitment process

The first step is to decide whether you have a vacancy to fill or whether you need to reallocate tasks among existing employees. Look at the job in the context of the organisation as a whole and in the light of likely future developments. Consult managers and other colleagues to help define the job and the kind of person you need to undertake it.

You may wish to recruit someone with specific skills, abilities or experience, but you may also be interested in looking for someone able to make a general contribution and flexible enough to change jobs within the organisation, if this proves desirable for the individual or the organisation.

Decide how you will attract candidates. If you have an HR department, it will be able to place an advertisement. Alternatively, you may wish to use an employment agency. Draw up a shortlist of preferred candidates but reply to everyone, perhaps keeping some applicants in reserve in case your first or second choice of candidates does not accept your invitation to interview or offer of a job.

2 Revise and use job descriptions and person specifications

Once the vacancy has been agreed, take a close look at:

- the principal purpose or objective of the job or role
- areas of and limits to responsibility
- relationships involved in the job
- the main duties and key tasks.

Consider also what will be required in terms of:

- education and qualifications
- experience
- skills and knowledge
- disposition and fit with organisational culture
- future career aspirations.

Keep the requirements of equality legislation and standards in mind and remember that diversity can be a positive advantage.

3 Draw up a contract of employment

Review any problems which may have arisen with existing contracts. Consider whether a short-term contract is preferable to a long-term one in the light of your plans and objectives. The right candidate may have their own preferences, so consider also the extent to which you would be able to accommodate these within commercial and operational constraints. Ensure that all legal requirements are met and consider whether to include additional clauses relating to the particulars of the post, such as mobility, home working, non-competitive clauses or planned job changes.

4 Prepare for and conduct the interviews

Good preparation for interview is crucial if you are to make the most of the opportunity to assess the candidates as accurately as possible. Systems and processes can be helpful in ensuring that all the candidates are treated fairly and consistently, but you also need to draw on your own interpersonal skills and professional judgement. Consider the following:

- the format and style of the interviews – one-to-one, sequential or panel, for example
- the environment, including seating arrangements – formal or informal
- the schedule – allow adequate time for each interview and plenty of time to prepare for the next
- the availability of appropriate documentation – application form, CV, person specification, job description
- a list of questions to ask – open, leading, probing and closed
- how you will listen to the candidate to pick up unspoken indicators
- how you will observe and assess the candidate's interpersonal and communication skills
- what salary and benefits will be offered
- questions that candidates may ask and how you will respond to them
- how to close the interview in a constructive and purposive manner.

As far as possible, be prepared to provide feedback to candidates who were shortlisted but did not receive a job offer.

5 Organise the induction

Once someone has been selected and appointed, plan a thorough introduction to the organisation as a whole, as well as the specific job. Induction is not just about informing new employees about their tasks and responsibilities, but also about helping them to integrate and identify with the culture of the wider organisation. Make sure that the organisation's principles, perspectives and priorities are explained in a realistic way, as well as providing details of organisational policies, procedures, standards and targets.

Don't try to cover everything on the first day, or even in the first week. Build in reviews during and at the end of the induction or probationary period to ensure that the new recruit has the best possible start.

6 Consider providing additional support

Some organisations run mentoring or coaching programmes designed to help employees learn about themselves and develop their potential. If these are in place, consider whether the newcomer would benefit from participating. More informal options might include assigning a colleague as a buddy to give advice and support to help the newcomer settle in. As appropriate, make the new employee aware of learning and development opportunities within the organisation.

7 Integrate the newcomer into your team

Remember that teamworking may be a new or daunting experience for the newcomer; that your team will have its own culture; and that newcomers must be introduced with care and consideration. Keep an eye on how things are going and watch out for any disagreements or issues between team members. Take care to explain established working practices and rules such as:

- decision-making and reporting processes
- where to find out about working procedures or who to ask if uncertain
- open and honest communication without fear of blame or recrimination
- flexibility of team roles – for example, if the leader is seen as a participating team member rather than just as the leader.

8 Empower your team

Empowering people is the surest way to gain their commitment, ensuring that mistakes and failures are not followed by blame or penalties. Empowering those who work with and for you means:

- being honest about your own opinions and attitudes
- being aware of the need for a culture of genuine trust and openness
- walking the talk and setting an example of how you want others to behave
- creating the right balance between encouraging employees to get on with the job and establishing the boundaries of responsibility and authority
- ensuring that employees have the skills and resources they need to contribute to team performance
- establishing effective, ongoing feedback based not on personality, but on tasks and performance
- listening to employees' views and giving them the opportunity to have a 'voice' in the workplace.

Recognise that – in the right environment – it is possible for people to cooperate with and support others in the pursuit of common goals, even if they do not have a natural affinity with each other. Building trust can also involve constructive conflict. Handled correctly, this can help bring emotive issues out into the open, resolve longstanding disagreements, enhance problem solving and act as an emotional safety valve.

It is also important to recognise and discourage destructive personal conflict. This can destabilise relationships, allow the polarisation of views and positions to develop, lead to negative and defensive behaviour, and create win/lose conflicts in which the emotional aspects become more important than the issue itself. Focus attention on tasks and actions in pursuit of common aims rather than on personalities.

9 Set clear objectives

Empowerment should not be an excuse for abdicating

responsibility. On the contrary, it is all the more important to set objectives that are SMART (specific, measurable, attainable, realistic and timely or time-scheduled). It is essential to clarify processes and levels of authority for decision-making. Appropriate measures of efficiency (how quickly you deliver) and effectiveness (how good the delivery is) also play an important role in meeting objectives.

Roles and responsibilities should be clearly defined and may need to be checked periodically. Make it your business to demystify, clarify and remove ambiguities. Remember that the employment relationship involves a continuous process of building understanding and trust to secure commitment and voluntary effort.

10 Appraise performance

A performance appraisal or review is a focal point for team members' learning and development. Ensure that appraisals are informed by evidence gathered by both parties during the period under review, not hastily put together on the basis of the most recent activities.

Appraising the performance of team members involves:

- encouraging self-assessment and helping with problem diagnosis
- offering help and suggestions that allow appraisees to determine their own solutions to problems
- focusing on specific tasks and activities rather than generalities
- getting a better understanding of appraisees' potential and development needs
- agreeing objectives and plans
- ensuring that appraisees have the resources they need to achieve the objectives set for them.

11 Coach for solutions, rather than dictating answers

Coaching is a proven method for developing skills, potential and performance. Coaching means working one-to-one with the learner to:

- establish the most appropriate approach to learning
- encourage the learner to experiment
- provide encouragement
- guide the learner with objectives in mind.

12 Reflect on how to motivate your team

The key to successful and consistent motivation is finding out what people want from their work. Recognise that individuals are motivated by different aspects of work – for example, more interesting work, greater involvement, greater recognition, better support, more opportunities for development, or just being better informed. Accept too that different learning styles suit different people: some like active involvement while others learn more from observation and reflection; some like to try things out while others do not like being thrown in at the deep end.

As a manager you should avoid:

- assuming that you have a job to fill without first looking at current workloads and job roles
- ignoring the legal aspects of recruitment and selection
- forgetting that starting a new job is a stressful experience for most people
- assuming a new team member will be fully integrated from day one
- assuming that the organisation may not need to adapt in some ways to integrate the new employee
- failing to give encouragement and praise when it is merited
- failing to address any people or performance problems that may arise
- neglecting the training and development of team members.

Organising the induction of new recruits

Induction is the process through which a new employee is integrated into an organisation, learning about its corporate culture, policies and procedures and the specifics of the new job. Induction should not be viewed in isolation but should be treated as an extension of the selection process and the beginning of a continuing employee development programme. Rather than limited to a one-day introduction, induction should be planned and paced over several days or weeks, marking the beginning of the new employee's personal and professional development within the organisation, and allowing the employee to integrate into the organisation. In the US, induction is known as orientation.

It makes sense – for both the individuals and the organisation – to help new recruits integrate as quickly as possible into their new surroundings and become effective and proficient in their work. Failure to do so can, at the very least, lead to erratic progress, with possible hidden costs such as waste of materials and loss of customers.

A good induction will help to minimise turnover of new employees and facilitate integration and subsequent productivity.

Action checklist

1 Review the positioning of the induction

Ask yourself whether your organisational or departmental induction does the job you require it to. Ask recent recruits for their views. Does the induction process achieve its objective of familiarising new employees with the organisation and settling them into the job? Check whether the induction is the end or the beginning of their learning with your organisation.

2 Check the scope of the induction programme

Does your induction include:

- a tour of the premises showing and describing the facilities
- an explanation of the organisation chart showing where the new employee fits in
- clarification of terms and conditions and health and safety information
- exposure to, and explanation of, the organisation's culture and values, departments, products and services, and a brief organisational history
- strategic objectives and business planning for the next operational cycle
- a clear description of the job requirements?

3 Appoint a mentor

Consider asking someone on the same grade or level as the newcomer to act as a friend and adviser for the first few weeks. This will be particularly useful in a large, complex organisation or in helping to explain details not fully covered elsewhere. Take the utmost care to ensure that the mentor is the right person, with the time to do the job as you would wish.

4 Plan the induction and involve and inform others

Ideally, an induction programme should be drawn up, and certainly authorised, by the newcomer's line manager. The mentor should also be involved in the process. Others who will be working with the new employee should be made aware of the induction programme, and whether or not they will be involved. The induction plan should comprise three stages: the first day or two should cover the bare essentials; the first three or four weeks should facilitate learning through a mix of approaches; and within three to six months the newcomer should have become familiar with all departments.

Take a look at the programme and check for variety, thoroughness and a balance of learning, practising and doing. Plan too to sit through several of the sessions with the new recruit.

5 Prepare the work area

If there is a long gap between a member of staff leaving and a new employee arriving, work areas and desks can become dumping grounds for others' unwanted materials. A few days before the arrival, make sure that the work area is clear, clean and tidy. First impressions count for a lot in the welcome you intend to provide. Check that all relevant stationery and office equipment is to hand and in working order. Don't forget the little extras like an internal telephone directory and perhaps a manual on how to use the phone system.

6 Introduce the recruit to the department and the organisation

On the first day, it is usually the HR department that informs the newcomer of housekeeping arrangements (catering, for example) and covers issues contained in the staff handbook, such as salary payments, leave arrangements and the sick pay scheme. Health and safety procedures will also be high on the list as they are a legal requirement.

Make sure that the new employee has copies of any necessary documentation – the organisation chart and job description, for example. This should be accompanied by an initial but clear briefing on the structure of the chart, the role of the newcomer and the fit between the two.

The new employee must also be introduced to the department and team in which he or she will be working. Although the newcomer will be introduced to people around the organisation at this stage of the induction process, a detailed look at what other departments do should follow later.

7 Emphasise the importance of organisational policies and procedures

New employees must be made aware of policies and regulations based on legislation, particularly in the area of health and safety, at an early stage. Other procedures based on national standards, such as ISO 9001 and Investors in People, and schemes such as internal employee development or mentoring programmes, should also be introduced.

Remember that it is easy for new employees to be overloaded with information on the first day of an induction and they will not be able to absorb or remember all the details of these procedures. Build time into the induction schedule for reading, assimilation and questions, and make sure that new recruits know where to find the information they need – on the organisational intranet, or in a departmental or personal staff manual, for example.

8 Plan a balanced introduction to the work

Whether learning and development are handled by the 'sitting-with-Nellie approach' or by professional trainers, a mix of explanation, observation, practice and feedback is advisable. Beware of information overload. New employees should be given some real work to do to avoid boredom and to give early opportunities for achievement.

9 Clarify performance standards

Make the performance levels you require clear from the outset. Employees cannot be expected to meet standards of which they are unaware. Where appropriate, discuss medium- and long-term needs and opportunities.

10 Conduct regular reviews of progress

These should be made during the induction programme, for example weekly, to ensure that the employee's objectives and needs are being met. It may be necessary to adapt the programme to match individual learning requirements and speeds. Reviews will usually consist of informal chats, but a more formal appraisal interview may take place at the end of the programme, particularly if the employee is on probation. The views of the employee on the overall induction process should be sought so that the design of future programmes can be improved.

It is not always easy to foresee how long the induction process will take. However good they are, induction programmes will result in a certain amount of overload, and important questions often arise after several months in the new job. Ensure that after the official induction is over there is someone to whom the newcomer can address further questions.

As a manager you should avoid:

- forgetting that starting a new job can be a stressful experience for many
- overloading the newcomer with too much information, too much listening and too much of the same thing at any one time
- making assumptions about the recruit's learning, assimilation and integration
- enlisting the services of an inappropriate mentor
- omitting to identify training or development needs at an early stage
- failing to review the new employee's progress regularly
- sticking rigidly to the programme if experiences – or expressed needs – are showing that the recruit's needs are other than expected
- omitting an overall evaluation of the programme at the end, or when the induction moves into a new stage.

Managing staff to mutual advantage

Mutual advantage means that both those who manage and those who are managed get the best out of the relationship. Workers benefit from knowing that they are doing their work well, that their contribution is valued and appreciated, and that they are using and developing their knowledge and skills. In turn, managers are satisfied that the tasks they have responsibility for are being carried out effectively, that performance is improving and that organisational goals are being met.

Good working relationships, based on mutual trust and respect, are the key to helping everyone in an organisation to give their best, realise their potential and pull together for the benefit of all. Ultimately, this will lead to increased job satisfaction and improve organisational performance, as people feel genuinely empowered to deliver. This checklist looks at the major building blocks for good relationships between managers and their subordinates and highlights the importance of being aware of changing perceptions of the role of managers and the nature of management.

Action checklist

1 Be aware of shifts in management practice

During the 1990s, many organisations started to move away from hierarchical structures, which tended to differentiate between workers at different levels, towards more flexible organisational arrangements designed to make better use of the skills and experience of their people.

There are a number of elements in this shift away from traditional working practices towards what is often known as the 'empowered' or 'flatter' organisation. This shift was between:

- the autocratic manager and the leader who energises his or her people
- authority by position and authority by merit
- domination and coordination
- control from the top and participation and collaboration
- self-advancement and self-development
- individual responsibility and the shared responsibility of teamwork
- controlling the workforce and giving them freedom
- power and empowerment.

With organisational culture firmly based on trust and initiative rather than on dominance, blame or fear, the onus is now on the manager to become a team member as well as the team leader.

2 Make change work for you

Be aware of the implications of change and its impact on individuals. For individuals, change will mean moving from the familiar to the unfamiliar, from the known to the unknown. Be aware of the effects that change can have on people, particularly when it is imposed. In leading change it is important to establish a climate of positivity rather than focusing on the negative or problematic aspects – this can help foster a readiness for change.

Psychologists have suggested that any substantial change in our lives involves a sequence of stages:

- **Shock** – emotional feelings of denial, confusion and disbelief, a sense that all around is crumbling ('This cannot be happening to me', for example). At this stage, offer understanding and acceptance of the state of shock, convey empathy, create opportunities for grievances to be aired and encourage the disclosure of feelings.

● **Withdrawal or resistance** – an attempt to keep the familiar world intact, a search for ways to avoid the consequences of change, a struggle to maintain the status quo. At this stage, counsel individuals to disclose their frustrations and anxieties. Listen with attentiveness and sensitivity.

● **Acknowledgement** – a sense of inevitability is accompanied by the recognition of a need to keep in step, a fear of isolation and rejection by others, uncertainty and insecurity. Help individuals acknowledge change by reviewing their skills, competencies and opportunities for development.

● **Adaptation** – this stage is reached when rational acceptance of change is matched by emotional and psychological adjustment. Inner confusion and uncertainty begin to give way to a more positive and constructive approach, as preparations for change take place, anxieties are reduced and practical steps forward are identified. At this stage, assist individuals by involving them in the design of new systems and procedures, helping them to gain familiarity with new resources and equipment, and getting them to propose new solutions and methods.

Different individuals move through these stages at different rates and in different ways. For some, certain stages are assimilated rapidly; for others, a particular stage can prove a great obstacle. Understanding the nature of individual behaviour provides a foundation for working with others and helping them get the best out of the constantly changing workplace. Most people will accept change if they see why it is necessary and are involved in the process.

3 Define the boundaries of responsibility

People who are new to a job have a high level of dependence on their line manager. This will normally diminish as they gain experience and learn the ropes. Allow them to feel their way and grow. As experience grows, the relationship changes and interdependence evolves. Situations will arise where the manager needs a progress report or consultation is required on specific issues. At this stage, encourage employees to report by exception and to present oral solutions to the problems they encounter.

Employees will develop the capacity to self-manage an increasing proportion of their job without supervision. Resist the temptation to interfere or over-supervise. Encourage independence and the responsibility that goes with it. These three elements – dependence, interdependence and self-management – are present in all jobs. Good practice involves recognising and responding to the shifting balance between them.

Whether you are working in a situation of rapid change or solid stability, in an empowered culture or one with a clearly defined hierarchy, it is essential to define the limits to the authority enjoyed by the people who work with you. For example, they cannot be wholly effective if they are confused about which decisions they:

- can take on their own, informing you afterwards
- can take only after consultation with you
- should pass on to you.

4 Identify your leadership strategy

If leadership is about quality and effectiveness, change and development, and focus on the future, the style adopted should be less to do with directing and instructing and more with supporting, coaching, motivating and delegating, so that people will own their work and be committed to it. A number of strategies can help in achieving effectiveness as a leader:

- **Management by walking around (MBWA).** Managers and leaders need to see their main activity as an interactive one, working alongside colleagues where tasks are carried out. MBWA is based on the belief that it is only by getting to know your colleagues and what they do that appropriate leadership can be provided.

- **Work review.** This is a non-directed relationship designed to help colleagues develop professional skills through the regular process of reflecting on their experience. Managing by exception reporting may also be appropriate – that is, setting a boundary within which the individual has freedom and reporting only when that boundary is in sight.

- **Critical friendship.** This concept is sometimes used to describe the nature of the relationship between a leader and his or her team. It is essentially an active listening role for the leader in which colleagues can explore and clarify aspects of their work experience. One-to-one discussion allows a deeper understanding of the work issues involved.

5 Give feedback

One of the most effective ways of developing others is to help them reflect on their experience in order to learn from it. Feedback is an informal and highly effective way of promoting this process. It is, however, necessary to be aware of some of the psychological implications of giving others information about themselves and their behaviour. Among the behaviours and responses managers may encounter are:

- difficulty in accepting responsibility for behaviour
- fear of making mistakes
- difficulty with uncertainty and change
- assuming that 'others know best'
- self-doubt and lack of confidence
- reluctance to set personal goals for development
- suspicion of 'experts' and those in positions of authority.

Feedback can be of three basic types:

- **Confirmatory** – giving people information that tells them they are on course and moving successfully towards goals. This type of feedback is vital but often neglected.
- **Corrective** – offering information that helps others to get back on

course when difficulties are present or things are going wrong. This should always be positive, not negative.

- **Motivating** – giving information that tells people about the consequences of both success and difficulties. This combines confirmatory and corrective feedback. The aim is to provide sufficient information to meet the development needs of the person receiving the feedback, enabling appropriate choices to be made and decisions to be taken.

6 Practise proactive passiveness

Getting the most out of relationships requires conscious attention at all times and can be challenging. Managers need to watch out for signs that those they manage (or maybe their team members) are experiencing feelings of inadequacy or excessive cynicism, have a sense of having 'plateaued', or are unable to express themselves.

While techniques such as MBWA, work review and critical friendship may involve substantial changes in behaviour to achieve the desired results, other more routine skills should become standard practice:

- **active listening** – where the listener attempts to gain insights into the perceptual, intellectual and emotional world of the speaker
- **giving undivided attention** – away from telephones and other interruptions
- **providing support** – using prompts and suggestions to check meanings, inviting the speaker to continue and otherwise keeping quietly interested
- **conveying understanding** – using body language to indicate understanding, acceptance and agreement.

Practice is needed in all of these. They need to become constant habits, not occasional events.

7 Review your relationships

Sit down from time to time and ask yourself: 'How are we doing?' Think through work routines and objectives so that you know where you stand in relation to others, and they to you. Focus on moving forward in such a way that the individual, the department and the organisation are all gaining mutual advantage.

As a manager you should avoid:

- being dictatorial, as this may create resentment
- forgetting to give credit when it is deserved
- not showing trust in your colleagues
- inflexibility in adapting your style to each employee
- always trying to have the last word
- being reactive rather than proactive
- being inconsistent
- failing to learn from your mistakes.

Ensuring clear communication

All communication consists of three elements: the 'sender' who originates the communication; the message that is being communicated; and one or more 'receivers' of the message.

Communication occurs when one person speaks or writes a message that is received by one or more other people. True 'communication' is not necessarily the message that the sender intended to send, nor is it necessarily the words that the sender used – it is the message that was understood by the receiver. Clear communication exists when the message received is the same as the message the sender intended to send.

Clear communication is critical to business and personal success, but it can be fraught with difficulties. This checklist provides an introduction to the basic elements of the communication process in general and outlines some principles that it is hoped will help readers improve their communication skills, both as the 'sender' (the speaker or writer) and the 'receiver' (the listener or reader) of messages.

Why is clear communication important?

- It improves efficiency in all activities.
- It reduces the frustration that arises from misunderstandings.
- It promotes clearer, more structured thinking.
- It involves putting yourself in another person's place, which

leads to enhanced understanding of other people and more effective management of relationships. This does not mean that relationships are necessarily more harmonious, although this may be the case.

What are the issues?

Communicating clearly can be surprisingly hard work. It is comparatively easy to:

- 'speak before thinking'
- send an email without considering the impact it will have or the impression it may make on those who receive it
- use words and phrases which mean something to you but may not be fully understood by others
- assume that the other person has the same background knowledge of the situation or issue as you do.

Why do communications go wrong?

- The message is not clear in the sender's mind.
- The words of the message do not adequately express the thoughts in the sender's mind.
- The words of the message are not consistent with non-verbal messages also being given out by the sender.
- The receiver does not understand the words of the message.
- Assumptions or prejudices in the mind of the receiver may hinder the correct understanding of the message.

Action checklist for senders

1 Prepare your message

Ensure that the message is clear in your own mind. What are you trying to achieve? How will you know if you have achieved it? Try to identify any assumptions you are making – about the other person's knowledge of, or attitude to, the subject, for instance. Look for any underlying prejudices affecting your view of the situation and the message you are trying to convey.

Think about your communication from the other person's perspective.

Ask yourself:

- How will this affect X?
- What problems might it give X?
- How does this fit in with what I know of X's objectives?
- How does this fit in with what I know of X's prejudices, likes and dislikes?
- Does X have the necessary background knowledge to understand the message?
- Will X understand any jargon or technical terms?
- Is this the best time and place to be communicating with X?
- What is the best way to communicate with X – write, email, telephone, or meet face-to-face?

Anticipate X's likely reaction, but do not assume that this reaction is bound to occur or be misled by wishful thinking. If your message is complex, plan and structure it with care.

It is not unrealistic to prepare consciously for every communication, but if your message is particularly important or is likely to be 'difficult', it is worth spending time on preparation. Consider seeking advice from a colleague. Ask someone to review drafts of any written communication and discuss it with them. Organise a dry run of presentations, interviews or conversations. If the content is confidential, use your manager or HR staff as a guinea pig.

2 Choose your words carefully

Check your understanding of any words you are not sure about, or better still avoid them. Misunderstood and misused words can be dangerous. For example, if I realise that I do not understand a word, I can ask for an explanation. But if I assume that 'continually' means 'constantly' or 'without stopping' and it is (correctly) intended to mean 'repeatedly', there is a problem. The message 'Evacuate the building when the fire alarm sounds continually' could become a recipe for chaos and disaster.

Remember the mnemonic KISS – Keep It Short and Simple.

- Eliminate unnecessary words. Avoid gobbledegook and keep sentences short. Your aim is communication, not literary elegance. Here are a few examples:
  - 'although' rather than 'in spite of the fact that'
  - 'while' rather than 'during the period that'
  - 'soon' rather than 'in the not too distant future'
  - 'I think' rather than 'the data appears to indicate that'
  - use short words – polysyllables are cumbersome.

- Avoid jargon unless you are sure the other person will understand it. The most dangerous jargon consists of words used in a technical sense which have a slightly different everyday meaning, as they can easily be misunderstood. Much management jargon falls into this category. Acronyms and abbreviations should also be avoided, or defined on the first occasion they are used. However, if you and your receiver understand the technical jargon, use it to make your communication more precise.

- Use positive phrases rather than negative ones – they are easier to understand as well as being more persuasive. For example: 'please call me if' rather than 'please do not hesitate to call me if'. Double and triple negatives can obscure your meaning. For example: 'There is no doubt that his request will not be granted' – well, will it be granted or not?

- Use concrete rather than abstract verbs and nouns. For example:

- 'sandwich bar', 'canteen' or 'coffee machine' rather than 'refreshment facilities'
- 'tell' or 'write to' rather than 'inform'.

● Use active rather than passive verbs for simplicity and clarity. For example:

- 'I think' rather than 'it is thought that'
- 'you requested' rather than 'it was requested that'

● Use 'I' language when you wish to give accurate, non-aggressive feedback or handle a difficult situation. This is more accurate and conveys the meaning more fully. For example:

- 'I don't understand' rather than 'what do you mean?'
- 'I felt let down' rather than 'you let me down'
- 'I particularly need the job by the deadline because' rather than 'don't miss the deadline'
- 'I support your decision' or 'I disagree but I am prepared to go along with your decision' rather than 'it's your decision'.

Be careful to avoid language that may cause offence or be construed as patronising or discriminatory.

Ask questions to seek information or direct a conversation:

● **Open questions** encourage the other person to answer at some length, expressing their views and feelings. They are often introduced by 'What?', 'Why?' or 'How'; for example, 'What do you think?' rather than 'Do you agree or not?'

● **Closed questions** should be used to elicit short, specific pieces of information, even just 'Yes' or 'No'. They are ideal for clarifying a problem or situation. For example 'When did that happen?' or 'Have you told your manager?'

● **Reflective questions** can be used to bring underlying feelings and opinions into the open, or to check that you've understood the other person correctly.

● **Statements** such as 'Were you pleased with that solution?' or 'You sound upset about it' can also be used to gauge feelings and opinions.

Leading questions are those where the question suggests the answer you want or expect to receive, for example 'May we conclude that …?' These are less helpful than other types of question, as you cannot tell whether you received the answer you expected because it was correct or because of the way you asked it.

3 Reinforce your message

It has been suggested that in any face-to-face communication, the words used make up only 10% of the message. It is certainly clear that body language – posture, facial expressions, gestures, tone of voice and non-verbal utterances such as grunts and sighs – play a significant role in communication. If your spoken words do not match your tone of voice or body language, the receiver is more likely to be influenced by these than by the verbal message. 'I agree' said with a clenched jaw, or 'What a great pity' spoken in a light, casual tone, convey the opposite message to the words.

When your message is not what people expect to hear, take particular care to match non-verbal communication with your words. Bear in mind that people often hear what they expect or want to hear.

To improve face-to-face interactions, try to 'pace' the other person's voice and body language. 'Pacing' is a delayed, understated matching of the other person's voice tempo and volume, body posture, gestures and facial expressions. This is a powerful tool for making communications more productive, and can reduce conflict, embarrassment and reserve. It does not mean you will invariably get your way, however. It may feel awkward at first, but it is a skill that improves rapidly with practice.

Remember the old training adage: 'First tell them what you're going to tell them; then tell them; then tell them what you have told them.' Providing preliminary summaries for complex messages and recapping for all but the simplest or least important communications will increase understanding and retention of your messages.

When a spoken message is important, confirm it in writing. Written communications are less likely to be misunderstood.

Action checklist for receivers

1 Prepare

You can prepare only if you are expecting a message – but this does apply to much business communication.

Try to put yourself in the sender's position. What are they likely to want to achieve? How important is it? Do be careful about any assumptions, however, as they can frequently lead to misunderstanding.

2 Listen

The receiver has as much responsibility for the success of a communication as the sender. Poor listening is a common communication problem. Causes include:

- the mind wandering – because your brain can think at a much faster rate than people speak
- fatigue or stress
- focusing on how you will respond to the message rather than on what is actually being communicated
- thinking about other things – perhaps because of lack of interest
- preconceived ideas and assumptions about what the speaker will say
- hostility towards the speaker.

A simple mnemonic, LISTEN, can help:

- **L**ook interested – maintaining eye contact with the speaker helps you to concentrate. An alert, interested expression will, believe it or not, make you feel more interested (in the same way that it is difficult to feel angry about something if you are smiling and laughing).

- Inquire with questions, to check your understanding. Don't make assumptions.

- Stay on target, using any slack thinking time to consider the implications of what the speaker is saying.

- Take notes, to help you concentrate and refresh your memory later.

- Evaluate the whole message, watching body language as well as hearing the words.

- Neutralise your feelings, acknowledging to yourself any prejudices you may have. Try 'pacing' the speaker yourself.

3 Read

Important material should be read carefully, but it is not always possible to read everything we receive. Some unimportant communications, such as junk mail, can be filtered out and binned unread. Some written communications can be scanned rapidly – reading the first sentence of each paragraph is an effective way of scanning a document, as these are often 'signposts' to the contents of the paragraph.

It is not as easy to check your understanding of written communications by questioning the sender as it is for spoken communications, but it is just as important. Points listed above such as taking notes and neutralising your feelings are relevant to readers as well as to listeners.

As a manager you should avoid:

- underestimating the cost of poor communication, in terms of money and relationships

- making assumptions without realising that you are doing so or checking them with the other person.

Team briefing

Team briefing is a process in which managers and supervisors talk to their teams to exchange information and ideas. The basic principles are that it:

- is face-to-face
- takes place in small teams
- is led by the team leader
- happens on a regular basis
- includes both organisational and team information
- offers an opportunity to voice concerns and suggestions that are taken seriously.

Team briefing originated in the 1960s when companies developed briefing groups, which cascaded information through the organisation. The emphasis then switched to the department or work group, where 'local' information of relevance to the immediate group was added to organisational messages and managers were encouraged to promote the flow of information in all directions – down, up and sideways. It is important to view team briefing as part of a wider internal communication strategy for ensuring that employees are well informed and have opportunities for upward feedback.

Team briefing:

- ensures people feel well informed
- provides opportunities for upward feedback

- develops trust, cooperation and commitment
- helps people understand change
- reduces misunderstandings
- reinforces the role of the team leader.

Action checklist

1 Gain the commitment of line managers

Team briefing depends on committed delivery and the ability of managers to listen to suggestions and concerns. Line managers should explain organisational strategies and reasons for change with conviction and tailor communication to local contexts. They should also listen to concerns and take action to ensure points raised are considered and a response provided.

2 Consult employee representatives

Involve trade union and employee representatives from the beginning of the process. Discuss the purpose of team briefing, encourage them to participate in the design of the system and reassure them that it is not a mechanism for undermining union influence.

3 Coordinate briefings

Team briefing should be coordinated by the department responsible for internal communication to ensure consistency and to collate upward feedback. The internal communication department:

- plans and structures the system
- provides the core briefing pack
- develops training programmes for line managers
- collates feedback and ensures it is considered by the senior management team.

4 Make sure that line managers are trained

Line managers should be trained in effective communication, as poor briefing undermines the process. The emphasis in training should be on the ability to present with conviction, to be clear, to encourage comments and suggestions, to be consistent in what is said and to act on upward feedback.

5 Logistics

Employees should be given time to attend team briefings. Remember that a willingness to cancel or postpone briefings when there are exceptionally busy periods or when team members are absent will be seen as a lack of commitment to the process. Communicating is part of the day job, not something you fit in when you can.

6 Team briefing structure

The department responsible for internal communication sets the process for team briefing. This is usually at least monthly with a simple process for capturing upward feedback provided.

7 Content of briefings

The Work Foundation recommends reports covering the four Ps: progress, policy, people and points for action. Start the session with the core brief and then discuss how this applies to the local team before going on to other local topics.

8 Allow opportunities for discussion

Ensure that time is allowed for discussion during briefings. Any questions that cannot be answered on the spot must be responded to within a guaranteed period.

9 Monitor the system

The internal communication department checks that team briefing is being carried out across the whole organisation and that core information is understood. Ways of doing this include:

- managers' walkabouts when team briefing is taking place
- employee attitude surveys
- feedback forms
- audits by outside bodies.

As a manager you should avoid:

- confusing team briefing with other processes
- allowing briefing sessions to develop into lengthy problem-solving workshops or an alternative to other team meetings
- imposing an off-the-shelf system without tailoring it to suit your organisation's specific needs
- launching team briefing without talking to the internal communication department
- assuming that only new information is appropriate or worth disseminating; frequently it is important to update earlier information.

Effective verbal communication with groups

This checklist covers face-to-face communications with all types of groups. Internally, these may range from large formal team briefings to casual encounters between two or three colleagues from different departments. External groups can involve, for example, suppliers, customers, competitors and regulatory authorities. In each context, managers may play a slightly different role, but the principles of effective communication remain the same.

As organisations become less formally hierarchical, it is increasingly important for managers to get things done by involving and cooperating with others, rather than by simply passing on instructions to junior employees. The ability to make things happen depends on adopting different roles, styles and techniques, and on being an effective member of different groups both inside and outside the organisation. These can include virtual and international teams with different skills and cultural roots.

An introduction to skills and techniques for oral communication with groups is provided here.

Action checklist

1 Define the purpose of the communication

Clarify the purpose of the communication at the outset; consider whether it is, for example, a meeting at which decisions need to be taken, a briefing session intended to impart information, or a brainstorming/mind-mapping session designed to generate new ideas. Some tasks, such as sifting existing ideas, coming up with new ideas or involving people in a key decision, are better done in groups. Others are best left to individual or written communications, particularly where there is a need to impart large amounts of factual or sensitive information. Whatever the purpose, you must be able to judge whether it is being or has been achieved and to steer the communication process toward this end.

2 The communication method

The communication method is worth considering. Increasingly this includes teleconferencing, and videoconferencing. Although both of these involve 'face-to-face' communication, there may be limitations in terms of the ability to 'read' others because of time delays or reduced non-verbal signals. There may also be a need to find some way to order the input so that all get a chance to participate.

3 Limit the extent of the communication

Set a time limit (even for an informal encounter) and an agenda (even if it is an unwritten one). Be realistic about what you can expect to achieve within the group, given those who are present, and be sensitive to the pressures on other people's time.

4 Ensure the right people are there

Group communication works best when all those present have a legitimate reason to be there, have something to contribute to the discussion and have an interest in the outcome. If the right people are unable to attend, postpone discussions rather than waste time on an inconclusive debate.

5 Get the right number of people

Five is recognised as the optimum number for effective debate and decision-taking in most group discussions. This makes it possible for members to adopt different roles, and allows a single member to be in a minority without experiencing undue pressure to conform. Getting the right people together, however, is always more important than getting the right number. If a larger group is unavoidable, consider using room layout to create no more than five subgroups and apply the same rules to each smaller group.

6 Prepare

Whenever the communication is pre-planned, make the effort to prepare and be familiar with the subject in advance. 'Winging it' is a dangerous strategy, especially when others have had the chance to prepare; it can also be viewed as insulting to others who have made the effort to prepare.

7 Facilitate introductions

If you are leading a group, make it clear what people's roles are, why they are there and what they are expected to contribute. If expectations turn out to be unrealistic, allow people either to leave, or to suggest other group members. As a member, define the contribution you expect to make and your authority for making it – for example, whether that authority is personal (a function of your own position) or vested (you have been asked to speak on behalf of someone else).

Set the tone for the language to be used. Will it be technical and specific or more general? The language of communication must be inclusive to facilitate good communication.

8 Be active

If you have agreed to be part of a group, participate actively. Take full responsibility for its success or failure, be energetic and make positive contributions. If you have nothing to contribute, admit it, and step down rather than waste the time of the other group members.

9 Be rational but open-minded

Take up a clear position on issues, but be willing to listen to rational argument and be prepared to change your mind. If you do change your mind, explain why. Groups work effectively only if participants are open to new information and different points of view.

Ensure that each member has the opportunity to speak, even if you have doubts about the likely wisdom of their views. Don't put your own ideas ahead of the group's overriding objective.

Be aware that someone may be 'quiet' if they hold a contrary view to others. Try to draw out their views without intimidating them or letting others intimidate them. A contrary view may be a breath of fresh air, stimulating further productive discussion.

10 Be aware of the dangers of unconscious domination

If the 'leader' always gives his or her views first, it is possible that others may:

- be unduly influenced from the start
- think that the ends are all 'sewn up' and they don't need to contribute, just react
- get into the habit of not thinking for themselves.

11 Guard against a tendency towards groupthink

'Groupthink' is a natural psychological phenomenon linked to group dynamics which leads those within the group to conform with the opinions of the majority. While compromise may be necessary in reaching a consensus, groupthink can result in false assumptions and poor decision-making. Reduce its influence over your input by defining your contribution in terms of meeting the group objectives, then stick to your position unless you are genuinely convinced by others' arguments. Have a genuinely open mind and keep on listening throughout the discussion.

12 Be brief, be simple and be organised

Speak slowly, clearly and directly in short sentences. Structure your arguments logically. Think about what you are going to say, say it and then summarise what you have said. Link your comments to what others have already said, and clarify areas of support for or disagreement with the positions of others.

13 Make good use of non-verbal communication

Use gestures to reinforce your key messages and non-verbal signals to convey attitudes and expressions. Make regular eye contact with each member of the group and use non-threatening but positive body language to convey an impression of calm and confidence. Pay close attention to the non-verbal signals of others. Ask yourself whether you are irritating or patronising members of the group and whether any are opting out of the discussion.

14 Stay calm and don't get drawn into arguments

If you believe a group is taking the wrong decision, stay calm and don't become emotional in defence of your own point of view. Stress points of agreement and minimise areas of disagreement, with a view to finding a way forward.

15 Avoid personal attacks

The key to effective group communication is mutual respect. When you believe someone is wrong, criticise their ideas by all means, but not the person. You should:

- keep any criticism constructive – for example, preface it with a word of support or agreement on a related topic
- resist any temptation to allocate blame – any attribution of blame for mistakes or failures is likely to lead to a breakdown in group dynamics.

While group members may be competing to present their individual positions, remember that you all need to cooperate to find an overall, acceptable solution which all will support and deliver.

16 Bring the communication to a conclusion

Review what you were expecting to get out of the communication and whether you have achieved this. Write up a 'decision and action' statement as soon as possible after the meeting and make sure all present have a copy. Give copies to any interested parties who were not able to be present, but be careful not to reopen the issue if a decision has been reached.

As a manager you should avoid:

- knowing too little about the reference points of other group members and how their view of an issue may create barriers to your own objectives

- allowing natural tendencies towards groupthink through which group members sometimes say only what they think the leader wants to hear

- dominating discussions and allowing your conviction of the merits of your own argument to blind you to the merits of the arguments of others

- allowing personal prejudices or assumptions, and consequent expectations of how particular group members will react, to affect you.

John Adair

Action-centred leadership

Introduction

John Adair (b. 1934), best known for his three-circle model
of action-centred leadership, is widely regarded as the UK's
foremost authority on leadership in organisations. Like Warren
Bennis in the US, he firmly believes that leadership can be taught
and that it is a transferable skill. Adair's ideas remain popular
because they are practical and relevant to managers irrespective
of working environment, and his works have been instrumental
in overturning the 'great man' theories of leadership. Adair is well
known for drawing a clear distinction between leadership and
management; the latter, he contends, is rooted in mechanics,
control and systems. He contrasts this with his teaching method,
action-centred leadership, which has proved to be an enduring
approach defining leadership in terms of three overlapping and
interdependent circles: task, team and individual. His other ideas
on the practical aspects of leadership, such as decision-making
and personal effectiveness, are less well known, although many
of them were ahead of their time and are now widely taught and
applied.

Life and career

Adair's early career was varied and colourful and undoubtedly
formed the basis for his views on leadership. After joining the
Scots Guards he became the only national serviceman to serve

in the Arab Legion, where he was adjutant in a Bedouin regiment. Before going to university he qualified as a deckhand and worked on an Icelandic trawler. He also worked as an orderly in a hospital operating theatre. After studying at Cambridge University, he became senior lecturer in military history and leadership training adviser at the Royal Military Academy, Sandhurst. He went on to become director of studies at St George's House in Windsor Castle, and two years later was appointed assistant director of the Industrial Society, where he pioneered action-centred leadership. In 1979 he became the world's first professor in leadership studies at the University of Surrey. A prolific thinker, Adair's academic accolades include Master of Letters from Oxford University, and a Doctorate of Philosophy from King's College, London. The prestigious title of Honorary Professor was recently bestowed upon him by the People's Republic of China for his outstanding contribution and research in the field of leadership. He currently acts as an adviser and consultant to a diverse range of clients in both the private and public sectors. Such clients include the Royal Air Force, the Royal Navy, the British army and the Scottish Police Service.

Key theories

Action-centred leadership

This simple and practical model is figuratively based on three overlapping circles. These represent the task, the team and the individual. The model seems to endure well, probably because it is the fundamental model for describing what leaders have to do, the actions they must take whatever their working environment, to be effective:

1 Achieve the task

2 Build and maintain the team

3 Develop the individual

Task, team and individual

Adair's concept asserts that the three needs of task, team and individual are the watchwords of leadership, as people expect their leaders to help them achieve the common task, build the synergy of teamwork and respond to individuals' needs.

- The task needs work groups or organisations to come into effect because one person alone cannot accomplish it.

- The team needs constant promotion and retention of group cohesiveness to ensure that it functions efficiently. The team functions on the 'united we stand, divided we fall' principle.

- The individual's needs are physical (salary) and psychological (recognition, sense of purpose and achievement, status). Individuals also need to give and receive from others in a work environment.

For Adair, the task, team and individual needs overlap:

- **Achieving the task** builds the team and satisfies the individuals.

- **If the team needs are not met** – if the team lacks cohesiveness – performance of the task is impaired and individual satisfaction is reduced.

- **If individual needs are not met**, the team will lack cohesiveness and performance of the task will be impaired.

Adair's view is that leadership exists at three different levels:

- **team leadership** of teams of 5–20 people

- **operational leadership**, where a number of team leaders report to one leader

- **strategic leadership** of a whole business or organisation, with overall accountability for all levels of leadership.

At whatever level leadership is being exercised, Adair's model takes the view that task, team and individual needs must be constantly considered.

The strengths of the concept are that it is timeless and is

independent of situation or organisational culture. Furthermore, it can help a leader identify where he or she may be losing touch with the real needs of the group or situation.

Leadership functions

To fulfil the three aspects of leadership (task, team and individual) and achieve success, Adair believes that there are eight functions that must be performed and developed by the leader:

1 **Defining the task.** Individuals and teams need to have the task distilled into a clear objective that is SMART (specific, measurable, achievable, realistic and timely or time-constrained).

2 **Planning.** This requires a search for alternatives and is best done with others in an open-minded, positive and creative way. Contingencies should be planned for and plans should be tested.

3 **Briefing.** Team briefing is viewed as a basic leadership function that is essential in order to create the right atmosphere, promote teamwork and motivate each individual.

4 **Controlling.** Adair wrote in *The Skills of Leadership* that excellent leaders get maximum results with the minimum of resources. To achieve this leaders need self-control, good control systems in place and effective delegation and monitoring skills.

5 **Evaluating.** Leaders need to be good at assessing consequences, evaluating team performance, appraising and training individuals, and judging people.

6 **Motivating.** Adair distinguishes six principles for motivating others in his book *Effective Motivation*: be motivated yourself; select people who are highly motivated; set realistic and challenging targets; remember that progress motivates; provide fair rewards; and give recognition.

7 **Organising.** Good leaders must be able to organise themselves, their team and the organisation (including structures and processes). Leading change requires a clear purpose and effective organisation to achieve results.

8 **Setting an example.** Leaders need to set an example to both

individuals and the team as a whole. Since a bad example is noticed more than a good one, setting a good example is something that must be worked at constantly.

Adair considers that these leadership functions need to be developed and honed to constantly improve the leader's ability.

Motivating people

In many ways, Adair's ideas on motivating people are in line with those of classical motivational theorists such as Abraham Maslow, Douglas McGregor and Frederick Herzberg.

The 50:50 rule

Just as the Pareto principle (or 80:20 rule) is the ratio of the vital few and the trivial many, the Adair 50:50 rule (from his book *Effective Motivation*) states that: '50% of motivation comes from within a person, and 50% from his or her environment, especially from the leadership encountered therein.'

Adair's view is that people are motivated by a number of complex and varied factors. So, for example, he does not dismiss the 'carrot and stick' approach, but rather sees it as one of the stimulus–response approaches that can be a factor, among many others, in motivating or influencing people's actions. For Adair, an individual's strength of motivation is affected by the expectations of outcomes from certain actions, but it is also strengthened by other factors such as the individual's preferred outcome (as demonstrated by Victor Vroom in the 1960s), conditions in the working environment, and the individual's own perceptions and fears.

Adair's eight rules in motivating people

Adair proposes that understanding what motivates individuals to act is fundamental to engaging their interest and focusing their efforts. The will that leads to action is governed by motives, and motives are inner needs or desires that can be conscious, semi-conscious or unconscious. In *The John Adair Handbook of*

Management and Leadership, he makes the point that 'motives can also be mixed, with several clustered around a primary motive'.

Adair emphasises the importance of a motivating environment and a motivated individual. The third, crucial, factor is the role of the leader who must, he believes, be completely self-motivated. In *Effective Motivation*, he outlines eight basic rules to guide leaders in motivating people to act:

1 Be motivated yourself

2 Select people who are highly motivated

3 Treat each person as an individual

4 Set realistic and challenging targets

5 Remember that progress motivates

6 Create a motivating environment

7 Provide fair rewards

8 Give recognition.

Developing a personal sense of time

Adair's view of time management accords closely with Peter Drucker's, in that he argues for the prior need to manage time in order to manage anything else. Adair was one of the first management thinkers to emphasise the critical importance of time management and its central role in focusing action and helping leaders to achieve goals. For Adair, time management is not simply about being organised or efficient, or completing certain tasks: it is about managing time with a focus on achievement. Time management should be goal-driven and results-oriented.

Success in time management should be measured by the quantity of productive work achieved, and the quality of both the work and the person's private life. The ten principles of time management given in *How To Manage Your Time* are:

1 Develop a personal sense of time

2 Identify long-term goals

3 Make medium-term plans

4 Plan the day

5 Make the best use of your best time

6 Organise office work

7 Manage meetings

8 Delegate effectively

9 Make use of committed time

10 Manage your health.

Of these ten principles, developing a personal sense of time, and thus increasing personal effectiveness, is central to Adair, again highlighting his emphasis on individual characteristics.

In perspective

It is perhaps unsurprising that there has been something of a backlash against Adair's thinking, given the pace and scale of changes in the work environment during the past twenty years. His ideas were novel when they first appeared, and for many people their main value lay in the successful challenge they offered to the then-dominant 'great man' theories. These theories, because they insisted that leaders were born and not made, undermined the possibility of training or developing people in leadership skills. Since Adair's views have been successfully established, however, he has become more of a target, with critics claiming that his approach (developed in the 1960s) has itself become outdated.

A major criticism of action-centred leadership is that it takes little account of the flat structures that are now generally advocated as the best organisational form. It is also criticised for being too 'authoritarian', applicable in a rigid, formal, military-type environment, but less relevant to the modern workplace, where the leadership emphasis is on leading change, empowering, enabling, managing knowledge and fostering innovation.

Another criticism of Adair's approach in recent years is that his approaches are too simple, are not academically rigorous and lack real substance, in that he is merely stating the obvious common-sense view. Others, however, believe it is this practical simplicity and clarity about what a leader should do that is so valuable – and timeless. For this reason, many organisations and business schools continue to teach the Adair approach to developing leadership. For over three decades his overlapping, three-circle model of action-centred leadership has been integrated into company cultures and individuals' leadership styles, and is an established hallmark of management training for many organisations.

The continued relevance of Adair's concepts for organisations today is reinforced by the republication of some of his principal works: *Leadership And Motivation: The Fifty-Fifty Rule and The Eight Key Principles of Motivating Others* (2006), originally published in 1990 as *Understanding Motivation*, and *The Art of Creative Thinking: How to be Innovative and Develop Great Ideas* (2007), first published in 1990. In addition, *Leadership for Innovation: How to Organize Team Creativity and Harvest Ideas* (2007) is a revision of his original work *The Challenge of Innovation*, again first published in 1990.

Adair has also penned two new works, *How to Grow Leaders: The Seven Key Principles of Effective Leadership Development* (2005) and *Effective Leadership Development* (2006), which strongly indicates the continued influence and importance of his ideas for inspiring leaders today.

Facilitating

A facilitator is a person who takes a non-directive, supportive approach to help individuals and teams develop, learn and find their own solutions, by creating the conditions for learning and constructive thought and using skills such as listening, questioning, posing problems and reflecting meaning in a supportive way.

Effective facilitators can help to improve communication and develop consensus within teams and groups. They provide non-directive leadership and support to assist teams and groups in understanding common objectives, identifying problems and finding workable solutions.

Facilitation also provides support to individuals, with the aim of building their confidence and enabling them to improve their performance and increase the efficiency of the overall organisation. Employees who feel supported by an effective facilitator are likely to become more participative, responsible and autonomous.

An increased reliance on teams and groups within organisational life has raised the profile and importance of facilitation, and global economic and social changes have created a growing need for managers and leaders to act as facilitators. A high level and variety of skills and knowledge are required, but managers will find that developing these will help them to be effective within their organisation and get the results they desire.

A facilitating approach will reduce employee dependency,

empower individuals, and increase staff involvement and empowerment, enabling work groups to be self-reliant and to function effectively and independently. Facilitation can also help to mitigate the impact of organisational politics and to manage partisan behaviour and conflicts. It can only work well, however, within an appropriate climate, where responsibility is reasonably devolved and a blame culture is strongly discouraged.

Action checklist

1 Understand the role of the facilitator

Be clear about what facilitation should achieve. The facilitator's role is to encourage others to talk, although in some cases the facilitator needs to steer the conversation into positive territory or towards desirable outcomes. A facilitator is there to influence the group, not to dominate it, and to support the dynamics of the group, not to dictate outcomes. The facilitator needs to tease out the key aspects of an issue or problem and ensure that any discussion or investigation explores as many avenues as possible, providing options that will help the group move forward. This can be done by being conscious of team and group dynamics and using a mix of questioning and listening.

2 Create an environment that suits your purpose

Start by creating the kind of atmosphere that will be most conducive to what you need to achieve, whether the context is a private interview or a group session, a formal meeting or an informal gathering. The ambiance should be comfortable, relaxing and non-threatening, for example, with the best room layout being either cabaret style for team-based interaction or a U-shape for larger groups.

At the start of each session remind participants of the ground rules of behaviour (switch off mobile phones, etc.) and the schedule, including the agreed comfort and coffee breaks. Stick to the agreed schedule, ensuring that the breaks are not missed and that the meeting finishes on time. Participants should understand that everyone has an equal right to speak, that all ideas are worthwhile and that speaking across others will not be tolerated. Make it clear what you will and will not do, and help the group to agree on an objective that can be achieved in the timescale available. One possibility is to ask participants to write their own ground rules and put them on a flip chart or PowerPoint slide to be displayed during each session as a reminder and a point of reference.

3 Develop empathy

Empathetic behaviour involves being 'with' people in their subjective feelings, problems and experience but keeping a part of yourself objective, so that you are able to offer support from a constructive perspective. Remain neutral, act as a mentor rather than a leader, and encourage others to take responsibility.

4 Skills for facilitation

Many different skills feed into good facilitation, including influencing and negotiating skills. The facilitator also needs the ability to:

- plan effectively
- run meetings
- set objectives
- assess situations accurately
- diagnose problems
- give effective presentations summarising ideas and suggestions.

It is also important that facilitators are able to recognise the potential of others and have an understanding of learning styles and experiential learning.

5 Questioning skills

- **Open questions** help to get people talking and exploring the issues. Beginning with 'How' or 'What', for example, is usually helpful here.

- **Probing questions** and **link questions** encourage more in-depth investigation of the issues.

- **Comparative questions** give individuals the opportunity to make a choice.

- **Hypothetical questions** can encourage discursive responses and allow you, as the facilitator, to assess levels of reasoning.

  Avoid **closed questions** that encourage simple 'yes' or 'no' answers as well as **multiple** and **leading questions**, which can cause confusion or lead to predetermined answers. Remember that facilitating is about enabling the participants to arrive at their own conclusions, so allow the conversation to flow freely, only intervening to guide it when necessary. Ideally, the conversation should be between delegates, not one-to-one with the facilitator.

  The facilitator is a neutral party whose job is to foster the emergence and sharing of information in pursuit of the session objectives. The facilitator's questions should reflect this aim. Often the challenge is to help the individuals express their ideas and knowledge clearly, and it can be useful to help individuals think through the details and/or consequences of what they propose.

6 Listening skills

The facilitator has the responsibility of producing a summary of the meeting and 'rolling-up' the discussion at the close. The techniques of active listening can help facilitators hear what was actually said as opposed to what they expected to hear:

- contact – connect with the other person, full attention and eye contact

- absorb – take in what is being said by the other person

- reflect – feed back what the other person has said

- confirm – elicit confirmation from the speaker that you have accurately reflected what they said.

  Similarly, ensure that others in the room are also listening – 'One conversation at a time please.'

7 Observe

To understand what is happening, the facilitator needs to be able to observe individuals and groups or teams carefully. A good facilitator should be sensitive to body language and the non-verbal messages that may be given or received, checking these out whenever necessary. Read between the lines and look for unspoken messages, nuances and disconnects, where the spoken word does not match the body language; this may indicate that people are saying things they do not believe to please others. Intervene when appropriate to move the discussion forward.

Body language can often be helpful, but equally people may make false assumptions, judgements and misinterpretations based on non-verbal messages. It is at this point that the facilitator needs a high level of emotional intelligence and awareness.

8 Paraphrase and restate

Paraphrasing and restating involve putting what is said into your own words and accurately reflecting it back to the group. This shows that you are listening and understanding what is being communicated, and also helps others present to be clearer about what has been said. Restatement goes beyond paraphrasing, providing a preliminary interpretation of the situation. The purpose of restatement is to check meanings and what you believe might be happening with the individuals or the situation. Be careful to do this diplomatically, especially if the topic is being hotly debated from different angles. A good facilitator will provide a balanced interpretation and focus on facts rather than persuasive suggestions.

9 Know when to keep quiet

Maintaining silence demonstrates effective listening and gives an individual time to think. Be patient, maintain self-control and eye contact, and demonstrate interest. Encourage people to take their time when they need to think about what they want to say. Silence can also be used to provoke truths and honest responses, as most groups find it difficult to sit in silence. If necessary, ask some brief questions after the silence to ensure there is no confusion.

10 Seek consensus and agreement

Seek to reach consensus and commitment to an action or decision by allowing time for questions to be aired, issues to be discussed and conclusions to be formed. It is important to ensure that all members of a group have an equal chance to put forward their point of view, and that discussions are not dominated by a few individuals. You may want to consider methods that don't allow particular individuals to dominate, such as using voting slips for decisions rather than a show of hands. Deal with disagreements and work towards a compromise when necessary. Do not be intimidated by difficult situations or people and be aware of groupthink – the answer may be as simple as suggesting a coffee break, or breaking into groups to consider an issue.

Facilitators need to be able to set objectives and keep people focused on the issue(s) under discussion, drawing them back to the point if the conversation becomes sidetracked onto minor or irrelevant issues. They may also need to encourage teams to generate ideas via brainstorming and other techniques.

11 Encourage a teamwork culture

Facilitators need a strong awareness of individual differences in areas such as cultural background, personality, ability, attitudes and how people behave in groups or teams. A teamwork culture should be encouraged to ensure that objectives are achieved, individuals are motivated and developed, and the team improves its performance. Open communication, team problem-solving and group decision-making will all contribute to a supportive climate.

12 Summarise and feed back

Summarising helps to reinforce what has happened or what has been learned, and to clarify the actions to be followed up on. Where appropriate provide feedback which will encourage team members and reinforce effective behaviour or help them to learn, develop and play a more effective role in group discussions.

As a manager you should avoid:

- taking a critical, unconstructive approach when giving feedback
- leading in a directive way, coercing group members, or contributing your own ideas
- taking control
- allowing a group to lose focus
- failing to keep an eye on the time
- assuming there is only one right, pre-empted answer or only one way forward.

Developing trust

Trust can be broadly defined as having confidence in the honesty, integrity and morality of another person, firmly believing that they will act in accordance with what they say. Trust has many aspects, including being trusted to maintain a confidence; having trusted abilities; being trusted to share the same aims; displaying judgement that people can trust; being trusted to give honest feedback; having trustworthy motives and ambitions; and being trusted to deliver what the boss wants on time.

Trust is a fundamental element of any relationship, including that between leaders and their people. Trust is the glue that holds relationships together. When trust is absent, leaders may find that their followers turn to someone else for guidance and direction. Trust is earned and built over time. It can take a long time to establish, yet only moments to destroy – and once lost, trust is extremely difficult to restore.

Trust is two-way: managers need to be able to trust their team to conduct its duties to the highest possible standards and delegate with confidence that the job will be carried out; and followers need to be able to trust their manager to lead them in the right direction to fulfil the objectives of both their department and the wider organisation. They have to be certain that the person leading them is not motivated by a personal agenda but has the best interests of the team and the organisation at the forefront of their decision-making. It is imperative that followers can trust their leaders to defend them when appropriate and can be sure that they are making the right decisions for the right reasons. Establishing a working relationship that is based on trust goes a long way to improving morale, motivation and employee engagement, which in turn leads to increased productivity and performance.

Action checklist

1 Be patient

Trust is not automatically present in a working relationship. It needs to be developed and nurtured over a period of time. The process cannot be rushed, so patience should be exercised until trust has been successfully built. Aim to cultivate trust slowly, ensuring that once you have it you are careful to maintain it. Never take trust for granted. Remember that trust is transient and can be lost more quickly than it is earned.

Developing trust will be particularly difficult if you are taking over a well-established team, especially if your predecessor was a trusted leader. Employees become familiar with the management style and behaviour of a manager, so inevitably the replacement of one leader with another will require a period of adjustment for both parties. In this situation it is crucial to convince your new team that you can be trusted, by showing them that you are in it for the long haul and are committed to delivering on your promises.

2 Demonstrate integrity

Integrity is an essential building block in forming a trusting relationship. You must be honest in your actions and your communications, showing that you are genuine in both. Be honest with yourself and with your team at all times, even when things don't work out as you may have planned. Freely admit when you are wrong or don't know something and reveal your vulnerabilities. This will go a long way to helping you become a trusted leader who is able to be open without fear of reproach.

Never under any circumstances should you lie, even if you feel you have already gained the trust of others. Lying is deceptive. This can have only a negative impact on relationships. Demonstrate your integrity by having the courage to act in accordance with your beliefs and principles, and let others see that you speak from your heart, not just your head. The importance of integrity increases with seniority, as others will expect to see you 'live' the values by which both you and the organisation are governed.

3 Communicate openly with your team

Communication is another fundamental element in building trust. Others will find it difficult to trust you if they feel that you are keeping something from them, or that you have some form of hidden agenda. Make your intent clear by communicating in a straightforward way, so that your words are not misunderstood or misinterpreted. Honest and open communication will effectively engage your staff. It is imperative that you are consistent in your communication. Communicating and cascading information will help your team feel that they are included and have the knowledge necessary to fulfil their duties. This will reduce feelings of vulnerability that can arise if they are 'kept in the dark'. If employees feel that the information you are cascading is accurate and timely, they are more likely to trust what you tell them. Communicate with the purpose of sharing knowledge; never deliberately withhold information as a means of control.

4 Get the job done right

For others to trust and believe in you as a leader, it is imperative that you demonstrate you can achieve what you set out to achieve. You may talk a good talk, but until you actually do what you say you will do, your team will find it difficult to believe what you say. If you are consistent in word and deed, you will be well on your way to becoming a trusted leader. It will take time to develop a track record, but aim to start as you mean to go on. By fulfilling the team's expectations of you, you will slowly gain credibility. This will help convince them of your ability to follow through on subsequent ventures and consequently gain their support. Take responsibility for your actions, admitting mistakes when necessary without being defensive, and apologise if necessary. When you can demonstrate that you have the ability to deliver what you promise, you will then begin to build a reputation as a successful leader, who can not only be relied upon to perform but, more importantly, can also be trusted.

5 Consider the bigger picture

To win the trust of others you must show that you have their needs, and those of the organisation, in mind. Don't focus exclusively on your own achievements and objectives. Others will find it difficult to trust a leader who is motivated solely by their own agenda. Let others see that you really care about them and the organisation and you will soon receive their trust and respect. By showing that you are driven by the wider organisational objectives, and those of your immediate team, you will help to develop a culture of trust which will hopefully continue long after your own tenure with the company. Let your team know what targets you have to reach and how this affects the department. They will see the positive impact you are making and understand that you are committed to delivering on your promises.

6 Don't abuse your position

Occupying a position of seniority within an organisation brings with it its own 'granted' power. However, do not use your status as a means of controlling your workforce, as trust cannot be gained in this way. Rather, delegate tasks to others and encourage them to take certain courses of action, as opposed to simply dictating to them. Use your position of power positively to make improvements that will benefit both your team and the wider organisation.

7 Show that you trust your team

The imposition of too many rules and regulations will send the message that you don't really trust your team. You have to demonstrate faith in their professional ability to conduct their duties according to expectations. By demonstrating your trust in them, they are more likely to respond to your faith in kind. Don't undermine your position as a trusted leader by needless employee monitoring. Instead, trust your team to take authority for their areas of responsibility and to make decisions commensurate with their role. Refrain from interfering with the work of others, unless you feel that their actions are detrimental. Aim to create an environment where trust is reciprocated so that you can effectively engage your staff and boost productivity.

8 Encourage the sharing of ideas

Your team need to be able to trust you before they will share their thoughts. You are responsible for the welfare of your staff and thus it is vital that they can trust you. Show your staff that you are genuinely interested in them, their opinions and their welfare and that you can be trusted to keep a confidence. Never betray a confidence or engage in tittle-tattle about others. Provide the opportunity for your staff to express their views and listen with genuine interest. Be open to the perspectives of others without being judgemental. Aim to create an atmosphere where people feel comfortable sharing their thoughts and ideas without fear of recrimination, even if they express opinions that are at odds with yours. Trust others to communicate and they will reciprocate by trusting you. You must also develop sound listening skills. Listening to the views and ideas of others will develop a trusting relationship, especially if you act upon their feelings and show that you are giving them just consideration.

9 Deal with poor performance

You must address poor performance in order to be credible to others. Be consistent in your approach to discipline, ensuring that you are fair at all times. Eliminate feelings of discrimination or favouritism. Trust and respect go hand in hand. Do all you can to ensure that this happens. Try not to develop a culture of blame. Challenge your team when necessary without being antagonistic, and aim to gain an understanding of their actions and their perspective, rather than blaming them.

10 Be consistent

Be consistent in your communication, actions, attitudes and behaviour. This will enable others to anticipate how you will react and respond in a given situation and reassure them that you will not act unpredictably. If you behave inconsistently, they will be unable to easily anticipate your reaction. This will make them suspicious and wary, and will develop a culture of uncertainty rather than one of trust.

As a manager you should avoid:

- 'talking the talk' without following through on promises
- betraying a confidence
- using authority as a means of control
- being inconsistent
- ignoring poor performance
- taking trust for granted
- forgetting that trust is fragile and can be destroyed more quickly than it can be earned.

Empowerment

Empowerment is a process whereby employees are given greater discretion to make decisions and act on them without referring to their superiors. Authority and control are shared to enable the organisation or department to function more effectively.

Empowerment requires the creation of a climate, atmosphere and culture that employees find safe and motivating and in which responsibility and accountability rest with the individual doing the job. It is also important to ensure that employees are provided with sufficient information and resources to carry out their empowered responsibilities. Empowerment is more than delegation. It should be a sincere attempt to redistribute power and decision-making responsibilities which strips away unnecessary bureaucracy while retaining agreed boundaries and reporting limits.

The introduction of an empowering style of management requires careful preparation and guidelines. If implemented successfully, the commitment and motivation of employees will be given a new lease of life, as they take greater ownership of situations, generate their own solutions and produce their own ideas for improving products, services and performance. Managers who are able to create an environment of trust, and energise, support and coach their people, are the key to successful empowerment.

Empowerment is an approach to management based on the belief that workers' abilities are often underused, and that employees can and will make a greater contribution if they are empowered to do so and are willing to accept the greater responsibility that this brings. Empowerment can reveal and develop people's talents, bring them closer to the centre of workplace action, and give them greater power and authority to innovate, participate in problem-solving and use their initiative. While there are clear benefits for employees, empowerment is an important management tool that will not only make the most of team members' talents but also save managers' time. Empowerment gives greater freedom to managers, who will spend less time making minor day-to-day decisions and thus have more time to deal with the 'big' issues and plan for the future.

Action checklist

1 Identify why you want to introduce empowerment

Clarify what you mean by empowerment and what you expect to get out of it. Is it an improved consultative process? Is it more active delegation? Is it extended responsibilities – with authority – for problem-solving and decision-making? Is your principal concern to develop people and expand their job capabilities? Or are you looking for improvements to the bottom line? Discuss what you have in mind and check whether the expectations of colleagues and senior managers correspond with your own. This will lead to unified and integrated outcomes.

2 Recognise the barriers to empowerment

Barriers may include:

- organisational culture – many organisations are inherently controlling, bureaucratic and unreceptive to change

- psychological factors – some managers may feel that empowerment means losing control, while some employees may not want increased responsibilities; and some employees may be scared of moving out of their comfort zone

- rigid routines – these often encourage people not to take responsibility

- specialisation – some employees may have a highly specialised or narrow job role which may lead to them seeing new responsibilities and ways of working as a threat

- poor information-sharing – some managers may be unaware or uncertain of what their teams know or have access to.

3 Be aware of the need for the right culture

There is no formula for the right culture, but it is important to recognise that some organisational cultures are more conducive than others to enabling employees to make a positive contribution, free from fear or blame. Consider the following archetypes, adapted from the work of Charles Handy (*Understanding Organizations*, 4th edition, 1993) and Edgar Schein (*Organizational Culture and Leadership*, 1985):

- **The role culture**, with defined functions and specialists and set procedures and job descriptions. This is suitable in a stable environment.

- **The task culture**, job- or project-oriented, concerned to bring together the right resources and people and let them get on with the job. Reliant on the formation – and dissolution – of teams, the task culture is better equipped than the role culture to respond to, and generate, change.

- **The fear culture**, where:
  - decisions, and truth, come ultimately from the more senior people
  - relationships are basically vertical and linear
  - each person has a niche which cannot be invaded
  - exchange takes place by agenda and prearranged appointment
  - there is deference to rank and authority
  - people use the formal communication process to 'cover their backs'.

- **The trust culture**, where:
  - ideas come from individuals

- people are responsible and motivated
- there is an air of informality and few closed doors
- people can make mistakes without fear of blame or recrimination
- there are constant opportunities for learning.

There are no magic tricks or techniques for changing an organisation's culture. It is a lengthy and an expensive process. Clearly, however, the culture of some organisations is more conducive to change than others, and this will include empowerment initiatives. A task or trust culture may well make the introduction of empowerment easier. In a role or fear culture it may be better to introduce empowerment in stages. Here it may also be useful to consider the work of theorists on change, such as Rosabeth Moss Kanter and Kurt Lewin.

4 Critically analyse leadership style(s) in the organisation

An important aspect of the right culture for empowerment is managers who adopt an appropriate leadership style. Empowerment may well involve making changes to your leadership style, so looking at some of the theories about how people lead may be helpful. The leadership continuum developed by Robert Tannenbaum and Warren Schmidt plots the relationship between managers and their team on a sliding scale, moving from a situation where the manager makes a decision and announces it to the team to one where team members make decisions within certain defined limits.

Tannenbaum and Schmidt suggest that leaders and managers should be aiming to move up this scale over time, thereby delegating more power to their employees. Like workplace culture, leadership style is not something an individual can change overnight. However, it is clear that moving higher up the continuum will enable employees to be better empowered.

5 Establish the boundaries

Although empowerment allows staff greater autonomy, there should be a clear indication of how far this goes, for example to the levels of consultation, participation or full decision-making. Set clear limits to levels of responsibility and autonomy. Wherever the cut-off is positioned, ensure that a mechanism is retained which allows employees to refer problems and suggestions upwards where necessary. Once the boundaries have been agreed and defined, reinforce them in practice by 'case law', so that team members learn when to do without telling, when to do and tell, and when to ask before doing.

6 Raise awareness

Before the process of empowerment begins, it is essential to raise people's awareness about what it entails. Set up meetings and discussion groups to let everyone know what is happening, why the process is being undertaken, what is expected of them and what the results are likely to be.

7 Reassure those involved and win support from others

Some people are bound to be more comfortable with empowerment than others. To understand your employees' motivation better, it may be useful to think about Maslow's hierarchy of needs theory. This identifies five broad categories of needs that motivate people, from basic physiological needs to the need for self-actualisation – feeling personal satisfaction for your achievements. Empowerment is likely to appeal to employees at this highest level of motivation.

Employees who are used to doing only what they are told, or carrying out only a narrow range of tasks, may feel threatened by or suspicious of a big change in culture. Allow people to air their anxieties and ensure they are comfortable with the processes involved. Good internal channels of communication are essential for empowerment, so keep these open and effective.

8 Evaluate current responsibilities and carry out an audit of staff skills

Do a job analysis. Find out what people do in their present jobs, and check it against both formal job descriptions and the implicit knowledge and skills used to fulfil the job role. Look out for areas where their jobs can be extended or where they are already unofficially empowering themselves.

Investigate the hidden talents employees may have. Ask people about themselves – do not just assume you know all about them. Draw up a 'talent rota' of underused talents, including those used outside the workplace. Think about how the opportunities now available fit with the skills and experience your employees have.

9 Ensure employees have sufficient information and resources to take control

Responsibility for customers, complaints and operational changes will need to be thought through, as will new responsibilities and the levels and types of resources needed to allow people to carry out their jobs. You will know that empowerment is working when customers become more satisfied, bottom-line results start to show through and people:

- seem able to run things without your daily/hourly involvement
- show initiative and take ownership of 'their' customers
- don't require you to solve 'their' problems.

10 Agree performance objectives and measures

Giving people real responsibility and resources to complete tasks is one thing; setting them adrift with these is quite another. Empowerment involves agreeing and establishing with employees the objectives and measures needed to ensure excellent customer service or a performance improvement that is also efficient and effective.

11 Launch the initiative

Employees may need a good deal of support in the early stages if they are afraid to take on extra responsibility – but support has to be distinguished from excessive supervision. Managers, too, may need careful handling, as some may perceive empowerment of their team as a threat to their control rather than an opportunity for improved processes and services.

Once the ground has been prepared, empowerment can start to take effect. Encourage the process by implementing or acting on new ideas that are suggested. To ensure success, it is essential to publicise what is happening and recognise and reinforce examples of good practice. You may find it best to start in an area where managers are known to be supportive and quick results can be expected. This will help to build momentum by showing how empowerment can work and will demonstrate your commitment to it.

12 Monitor and support developments

To ensure that empowerment succeeds in the long term, employees must feel supported in their day-to-day work. Regular meetings and one-to-ones can be used to check on progress, give and receive feedback, and gather ideas and support. If empowered employees have done their job well, this will reinforce their good performance. If they have fallen short in some way, this is an opportunity to discuss how future work could be improved. You should be specific and focus on the task not the person when giving feedback, especially if it is negative.

Consider how to maintain communication and highlight successes in order to build momentum and keep the initiative going. Be prepared to live with mistakes. As long as the same ones don't keep happening, mistakes can be useful learning experiences for the future.

As a manager you should avoid:

- seeing empowerment as a threat rather than an opportunity
- creating expectations that cannot be fulfilled
- failing to recognise or reward people who take on extra responsibilities
- going to extremes – either micromanaging or abdicating all responsibility.

Effective delegation

Delegation is about entrusting others with appropriate responsibility and authority for the operation and/or accomplishment of certain tasks or activities. More simply, it is about getting someone else to do part of your job – a job that is your responsibility but need not be done by you. Delegation does not mean getting someone to do work which is already a part of their job. Also, delegation should be positive – used as a means, for example, of developing employees, rather than just passing on work you do not like doing yourself.

Delegation is a crucial management skill, but many managers do not delegate effectively. This can be through fear of letting go or the mistaken belief that nobody else can do the job as well as they can. Sometimes it may be because they feel there is simply not time to delegate a task, and it is easier to do it themselves. The key is to make sure that you delegate, but without abdicating or interfering.

Effective delegation will free up your time, help with prioritising your work, and provide a means of developing your employees and assessing their potential. It will motivate individuals who get to do more challenging work for you and increase the skill levels within your team. It will also help with succession planning, as it will enable people to experience different levels of work.

There are various levels of delegation. An activity can be delegated without accountability, in which case you remain responsible for the outcome, getting the credit if the delegation is effective or the criticism if not.

Alternatively, you can delegate responsibility and authority for the activity, leaving the person concerned to get on with it. If you take this route, however, it is important not to abdicate completely. Try to maintain a fine balance between interference and neglect, giving interest, support and motivation to the employee concerned.

There are no real disadvantages to delegation if it is handled well, but it will take time and effort on the part of delegating managers and will involve a level of risk, in that the buck will still stop with the person who delegates.

Action checklist

1 Be consistent

Ask yourself whether you are delegating a particular activity on a one-off basis, or as part of a general framework for assigning activities to others and developing their skills. It is important to be consistent so that employees understand what to expect and a climate of trust starts to build.

It is important to work out – with your boss as well as with those who report to you – the boundaries of responsibility that enable your people to take a decision:

- on their own with no need to report to you
- and then report to you
- only after discussion with you.

Vagueness about boundaries of responsibility is common and is the cause of much confusion in organisations.

2 Identify the activity to be delegated

Be clear about what you want to delegate. Ask yourself what end result you want (in terms of people development as well as activity) and use this as the basis for deciding what to delegate.

Delegate whole activities rather than parts. If you delegate the whole activity, it raises the motivation level of the person carrying it out, develops them and helps them to really understand the job.

3 Think through the benefits of delegation

Clarify for yourself exactly what the benefits of delegation will be. Think through how it will benefit:

- you
- the person to whom you are delegating the activity
- the team
- the department
- the organisation
- the customers.

Only when you are clear about the benefits to most or some of these will you be able to sell the idea that it is worthwhile for the individual to take on the delegated activity. The act of explaining the activity is one of the main ways of gaining commitment to it, so you need to be clear about the benefits even at this early stage. But equally, try to assess potential problems:

- What might happen if things go wrong?
- What is the worst-case scenario for the team, the organisation, or the customers?
- What negative impact might this have on the individual?
- How much support should you give?

4 Identify the person

Make sure you are not too one-dimensional when selecting the right person for the job. It is all too easy to choose someone you have chosen before. Start afresh with a clean piece of paper and work through what the job is and the skills and attributes required. Ask yourself whether you want someone, for example:

- who is reliable and has plenty of experience

- who will take a risk but bring about a quick result
- whose development will benefit from the challenge
- who will simply absorb the workload as a matter of routine.

5 Negotiate the delegated activity

Delegation works best when the person taking on the activity fully understands what is required and is enthusiastic and willing to do it.

This process may need to be carried out in minute detail. If you are delegating the writing of a report, for example, you may need to specify the way the information should be presented, the arguments or hypotheses to put forward, and even the number of pages it should contain.

Sit down with the individual and come to an agreement about what they are going to do, when they are going to do it, what resources they will need and the outcome that is expected.

Sell the benefits to the person. Explain exactly what's in it for them and check they are happy to do it. Draw out the delegate's thoughts or fears and take account of these as you clarify and agree goals. Remember that the employee has the right to say 'no', and if they do, you must try not to hold this against them.

6 Allocate time and be supportive

Allocate the right amount of time. Agree a schedule and arrange to meet and compare notes. After a few weeks, check how the activity is going.

Remember that you are not just dumping work on them – you are working with them to make sure they can carry out the work that is required. Make sure that you are available so that they can talk to you if they have a problem or need advice.

7 Work out the right level of responsibility and authority

If you are delegating a part of your job which needs authority, make sure that the delegate knows they have your full support, and that other people in the organisation are aware of this too. If the delegated activity involves other sections, make sure that the appropriate people understand what is happening, why and with whose authority.

8 Make it happen

The routes by which delegates achieve what is required are up to them.

Do not specify how the job has to be done. Remember you have just delegated an activity – it is up to the person concerned to come up with the best way of making sure that it happens. Allow the person to get on with the delegated activity and complete it. Once you have provided the resources they need to do the job, make sure you do not interfere but are there to support them.

9 Review and evaluate

When the activity has been completed, carry out a review to see how well it went. Evaluate the positive outcomes in terms of the activity and the skills or learning which have accrued. Be constructive about any failures and try to establish what could be done better next time, for yourself as much as for the person to whom you delegate.

As a manager you should avoid:

- giving people tasks without supporting and monitoring their progress
- dictating how the job should be done
- choosing the same individual every time you delegate a task
- failing to credit the responsible person when delegated work is completed.

Setting SMART objectives

An objective is a statement that describes what an individual, team or organisation is aiming to achieve. Objectives are SMART if they are specific, measurable, achievable, realistic and timely (or time-bound).

Objectives set out what a business is trying to achieve. It is important for leaders and managers to get the process of setting objectives right, as inadequately formulated objectives could guide an individual, a team or an organisation in the wrong direction. Specific and measurable objectives provide a definition of the success of a project or initiative. Achievable and realistic objectives engage and motivate individuals. Time-bound objectives ensure that all stakeholders agree on when they are to be achieved.

SMART is an acronym that has been credited to both Peter Drucker (1955) and G. T. Doran (1991), though it is difficult to identify whether either of these two was really the first person to use the term with reference to objectives. The SMART concept is now commonly used by managers to set objectives within appraisal and performance management systems:

- **Specific.** Outline in a clear statement precisely what is required.
- **Measurable.** Include a measure to enable you to monitor progress and to know when the objective has been achieved.
- **Achievable.** Objectives can be designed to be challenging, but it is important that failure is not built into them. Employees and managers should agree objectives to ensure commitment to them.

- **Realistic.** Focus on outcomes rather than the means of achieving them;

- **Timely or time-bound.** Agree the date by which the outcome must be achieved.

Action checklist

1 Specific

Objectives should be specific. They should specifically describe the result that is desired in a way that is detailed, focused and well defined.

To be specific, an objective should include a description of a precise or specific behaviour, achievement or outcome which is, or can be related to, a percentage, frequency, rate or number.

To increase specificity when writing objectives, use action-oriented verbs to describe the actions that need to be taken to fulfil the objectives.

Action verbs include:

- analyse
- apply
- change
- create
- determine
- differentiate
- identify
- perform.

Avoid jargon, words and phrases which are (or can be construed as) misleading or ambiguous, such as:

- be aware of
- have an awareness of

- be prepared for a variety of.

  To help set specific objectives ask:
- What are we going to do, with or for whom?
- How will this be done and what strategies will be used?
- Why is it important that this is done?
- Is the objective (or objectives) understood?
- Is the objective (or objectives) described with action verbs?
- Who is going to be responsible for what, and do we need anyone else to be involved?
- Where will this happen?
- When do we want this to be completed?
- What needs to happen?
- Is the outcome clear?
- Will this objective lead to the desired results?

2 Measurable

Measurement is hugely important. Evidence derived from a system, method or procedure which has tracked and recorded the behaviour or actions upon which the objective is focused will tell you whether the objective has been achieved or not.

Consider:

- How will I know that the change has occurred?
- Can these measurements be obtained? It is worth noting that if it can't be measured now, the chances are that it won't be possible to measure it in the future either.

3 Achievable

Objectives should be achievable. They can be stretching but not unachievable. Ask whether, with a reasonable amount of effort and application, the objective is achievable.

An objective is achievable if:

- you know that it is measurable
- others have already done it
- it is in principle possible – it is clearly not unachievable
- the necessary resources are available, or there is a realistic chance of getting them
- the limiting factors and/or risks have been assessed.

Setting objectives that are unachievable will lessen motivation and lead to people applying little or no energy or enthusiasm to what they see as a futile task. Setting objectives at too low a level, however, can be just as dispiriting.

Recognise that by declaring an objective to be achievable you may be making a commitment to provide a level of resources (employees, money, etc.) without which the objective would not be achievable, implying that in changed circumstances the objective would no longer be SMART for the individual, team or organisation.

4 Realistic

Objectives should be realistic, but this does not mean that they need to be easy. They can stretch the individuals, teams or organisations responsible for the achievement of them. You can set objectives that are demanding, but not to the extent that the chance of success is small. Realistic objectives take into account the available resources, such as skills, funding and equipment.

You need to know:

- Is it possible to achieve this objective?
- Who is going to do it?
- Do they have the necessary skills to do the task well?
- Where is the funding coming from?
- Are the resources to achieve this objective available?
- Who will bear responsibility for what?

5 Timely or time-bound

A deadline, date or time when the objective will be accomplished or completed must be set so that it is possible to judge whether the objective has been achieved on time. It also facilitates the planning and scheduling of the process by which the objective will be achieved.

A deadline helps create the necessary urgency, prompts action and focuses the minds of those who are accountable for the commitments that they have made through the objectives. Not setting a deadline reduces the urgency of the tasks and the motivation of those required to perform them.

Ask yourself whether the objective can be accomplished within the deadlines that have been established, bearing in mind other possible competing demands that may cause delays.

The objective-setting process can seem intimidating, but this doesn't need to be the case; it can be as simple as scrutinising the departmental aims and considering how they can be met. Everyone within the organisation should have a clear understanding of the objectives as well as an awareness of their own roles and responsibilities in achieving them.

As a manager you should avoid:

- failing to set objectives which are specific
- having no system, method or procedure in place to track and record the behaviour or actions upon which an objective is focused
- setting objectives which are unachievable
- setting objectives which are unrealistic
- failing to set time frames for the achievement of objectives
- setting deadlines which are neither achievable nor realistic
- forgetting that situations may change and that objectives may need to be renegotiated if this makes achieving them less certain or impossible.

Face-to-face communication for interviews and meetings

Face-to-face communication is a process of personal interaction during which messages – including ideas, opinions, information, feedback, instructions, feelings and so on – are passed from one person to another. Within an organisation face-to-face communication takes place in many different contexts for many different reasons. It may be upwards, with your own boss or other senior staff; downwards, with junior staff who report to you or to other managers; or sideways, with colleagues. Externally, face-to-face communications cover a range of encounters, from those with suppliers, clients or customers, to those with colleagues from similar organisations or competitors. Effective communication means that the messages have been correctly received and understood and will be acted on appropriately.

Effective face-to-face communication is a crucial element in personal and organisational success. A few well-chosen words can make the difference between a message that is rejected or misconstrued and one that is clearly understood and achieves its purpose. Similarly, the time and place chosen for the delivery of a message, the approach taken or the tone of voice used can have a powerful impact on the response it elicits. This checklist provides pointers to the main factors affecting interpersonal communication in a range of organisational contexts and gives practical guidance on making your communications as effective as possible. In this age of remote communication and social networking, it is worth noting that attitudes to face-to-face communication are changing. Bear this in mind if you need to communicate effectively with younger employees.

Action checklist

1 Clarify the purpose of the communication and its expected outcome

Think about what you expect to achieve from the encounter. Distinguish between your long-term goal (for example to ensure that a major project is delivered on time and within budget) and what you expect to achieve from this particular meeting. This will provide a benchmark against which to judge whether the communication was effective. Practitioners of neuro-linguistic programming, which examines how thoughts and feelings learn to respond to language, use an effective set of questions before a communication:

- What do I want to happen as a result of this interaction?
- How will I know whether this is starting/going to happen? What will I:
  - see the person doing
  - hear the person saying
  - feel about the atmosphere?

2 Choose the time and place

Choose a time when the person you need to speak to will be able to give you their full attention. Don't raise an important matter that needs consideration at a time when the other person is under pressure to meet a deadline or is expected at a meeting elsewhere. Consider the most appropriate setting for the meeting, the level of privacy required and the facilities you might need. If you are fixing a time and place in advance, make sure that both parties are happy with the arrangements. Be realistic and set a time limit within which you can reasonably expect to achieve your planned outcome. With open-ended communications, such as counselling interviews, discuss the timing with the interviewee first.

3 Prepare yourself

Decide how much of the communication you can plan in advance. Do this where the outcome is known and critical and needs to be unambiguous. This includes, for example, contract meetings with clients or suppliers, disciplinary interviews with junior staff and critical progress meetings with senior staff. Take an unstructured approach only when the purpose of the communication is to seek information or to counsel. In some cases, you may need to gather relevant information or put appropriate documentation together.

4 Consider your use of space

Respect the personal space of those with whom you are communicating and think about the physical distance that will be appropriate to the context: too close and you will be intimidating; too far away and you could appear remote. If you need to compete, negotiate or argue, you may wish to adopt an assertive stance, positioning yourself directly opposite the other person; but if you are seeking cooperation and collaboration, you may want to sit beside them. Think too about the layout of the room where the encounter or meeting is to take place and decide whether a formal or an informal setting will be more conducive to success. However, be wary of using your desk as an artificial barrier to reinforce your status.

5 Ensure you are in the right role to achieve the outcome you want

Assume the role you need to adopt to secure your outcome, such as tutor, adviser, boss or salesperson. Do this consciously and don't slip into another role during the meeting or allow yourself to be led into one. Ensure you select an appropriate role: don't attempt to discipline someone if you have assumed the role of friendly adviser. Only change roles if the outcome you are seeking changes during the meeting.

6 Create rapport before you begin

Do what you can to establish rapport before launching into your pitch. Smile and enquire how the respondent is feeling. Ask questions that will encourage the flow of conversation before addressing the topic of concern. Be aware that people may be inhibited even if they appear at ease, especially if you are in a senior position. Try to establish that you are someone they can do business with.

7 Adopt the right tone

Use a tone that is appropriate to the role you need to play without appearing artificial. If you are seeking information, be relaxed, open and warm; if you are conducting a disciplinary interview, be firm and businesslike. Using the wrong tone or style will send a confusing message to the listener.

8 Set the scene

Begin by providing background to the issue to be discussed and summarising previous meetings or conversations. Ask for an update or new information and avoid second-guessing what the other person will say. Present your case openly and don't be devious or clever. Aim to focus the minds of both sides on the factual issues before progressing to remedial action or a solution to a problem.

9 Be aware of attitudes, values and expectations

Be aware of the other person's viewpoint and take into account what you already know about their behaviour and approach, especially if you are aware of the results of any psychometric assessments undertaken. Ask yourself how the person may view the issue and what barriers will this throw up to prevent you achieving the outcome you desire. You can use this knowledge to plan and steer the interaction. For example, a person whom you know to be factual, withdrawn and driven by detail is unlikely to be comfortable or motivated to act if you speak in an overly extrovert and passionate style. Consider their values and show respect at all times, but be wary of introducing prejudice by assuming that all employees in a certain category will view an issue the same way

10   Understand and manage the pressures both parties are under

Be aware of any possible concerns the other person might bring to the encounter that could block progress – their competence to do a job, their career prospects, what colleagues might think, or whether they might be asked to rush a job and compromise on quality, for example. Recognise and face up to the pressures on you – the need to act fairly, legal requirements, deadlines and time pressures.

11   Use the right skills to achieve the outcome you want

Strike the right balance between asking open questions to elicit information, particularly at the beginning of the interview, and more specific questions to tie down details. Listen carefully to what the other person says. Be aware of their body language and non-verbal signals, and use these to check that your questions are being understood and correctly interpreted. Use signals and gestures to reinforce your message and convey shades of attitude and expression.

12   Bring the encounter to a close

Actively steer the encounter towards a conclusion. Use closed questions to check your understanding and assumptions. Identify the main points the other person has made and use their words to summarise the main conclusions.

13   Stop once you have achieved the desired outcome

If you have set a clear objective for the meeting and achieved it, then stop. Don't dilute the impact of what you have said by straying on to another agenda or reviewing the content of the meeting. Being tightly focused on the outcome of a communication will gain you time and effectiveness.

As a manager you should avoid:

- trying to address an important issue at a casual encounter when time is short

- setting an overambitious agenda for a face-to-face meeting – you will confuse the other person and end up not achieving any of your objectives

- adopting the wrong role or style for an encounter or allowing yourself to be led into one that is inappropriate.

Abraham Maslow
The hierarchy of needs

Introduction

Abraham Maslow (1908–70) was an American psychologist and behavioural scientist. He spent part of his career in industry as well as working as an academic. His hierarchy of needs theory was first presented in 1943 in the US *Psychological Review* and later developed in his book *Motivation and Personality*, first published in 1954. His concepts were originally offered as general explanations of human behaviour but quickly became a significant contribution to workplace motivation theory. They are still used by managers today to understand, predict and influence employee motivation.

Maslow was one of the first people to be associated with the humanistic, as opposed to a task-based, approach to management. As people have increasingly come to be appreciated as a key resource in successful companies, Maslow's model has remained a valuable management concept.

The hierarchy of needs

Maslow saw human needs in the form of a hierarchy, ascending from the lowest to the highest. When one set of needs is satisfied it ceases to be a motivator; motivation is then generated by the unsatisfied needs in the hierarchy. The needs are: survival or physiological needs, safety or security needs, social needs, ego-status needs and self-actualisation needs. If managers can recognise which level of the hierarchy a worker has reached, he or she can motivate the employee in the most appropriate way.

Today the hierarchy is usually represented as a triangle, although Maslow himself did not present it in this way.

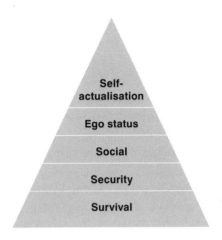

Figure 2: Maslow's hierarchy of needs

The hierarchy has five levels:

- **Survival or physiological needs.** The most primitive of all needs consisting of the basic animal requirements such as food, water, shelter, warmth and sleep.

- **Security or safety needs.** In earlier times these needs were expressed as a desire to be free of physical danger. This need has been refined so that its implications are now felt in terms of social and financial, such as job security, rather than purely physical requirements.

- **Social needs.** To belong and be accepted by others. Humans are essentially social beings and therefore seek membership of social groups, such as work groups.

- **Ego-status needs.** To be held in esteem by both oneself and others. This kind of need is satisfied by power, prestige and self-confidence.

- **Self-actualisation needs.** To maximise one's skills and talents. This embraces self-realisation, self-expression and self-fulfilment.

There are certain conditions, Maslow wrote, which are immediate prerequisites for satisfying needs, such as freedom to speak, freedom to express or defend oneself, justice, fairness and honesty. Danger to these is perceived almost as if it were a danger to the needs themselves.

The hierarchy is usually referred to as if it was a fixed order, but Maslow explained that it is not necessarily rigid or universally applicable. While most people do have basic needs in the order indicated, there are a number of exceptions. Creative people, for example, are often driven by self-actualisation rather than lower needs.

The hierarchy is often presented in simplified terms, giving the false impression that one need must be fully satisfied before the next one emerges. But as Maslow explained, humans are continually wanting animals, whose basic needs are partially satisfied and partially unsatisfied at the same time. Needs continually overlap; for example, social needs are felt by everyone, including those whose basic needs are not met. However, as soon as one need is satisfied it ceases to be a motivator.

Peter Drucker pointed out in his book *Management: Tasks, Responsibilities, Practices* (1973) that while it becomes less satisfying to obtain economic rewards as you move up the hierarchy, such needs do not become less important. This is because as their impact as a positive incentive decreases, their ability to create dissatisfaction and act as a disincentive increases. Economic rewards become entitlements and if they are not looked after can act as deterrents.

In perspective

Maslow is often mentioned in connection with his contemporaries, Douglas McGregor and Frederick Herzberg, who were also developing motivation theories at about the same time. Maslow admired McGregor, the author of *Theory X and Theory Y*, although he had strong reservations about the validity of theory Y. Herzberg put forward the idea of separating hygiene factors – those that can lead to job dissatisfaction (such as working conditions, salary, or company policy) – from motivators – those that lead to job satisfaction (such as achievement, recognition, responsibility, or advancement). Herzberg's hygiene factors can be compared with Maslow's levels one, two and three, and the motivators to levels four and five.

Academics have found little evidence to support Maslow's theory. His influence continues, however, through the work of later psychologists and writers, such as Chris Argyris, Robert Blake and Jane Mouton. Argyris looked at how individual initiatives and creativity can coexist with organisational rules. Blake and Mouton created the managerial grid model, which introduced the concept of the manager who balanced a concern for people with a concern for task.

Practising managers have found Maslow's theory a valuable and sensible concept which clarifies their thoughts. It is often used as a basis for questionnaires and checklists to discover an individual's level of motivation or as a basis for empowerment. In her book *How to Motivate People* (1988), Twyla Dell listed the ten qualities that people most want from their jobs and included two questionnaires to help readers judge how many of these qualities they were receiving and giving in their work. She then matched the ten qualities to Maslow's hierarchy.

Maslow's theory only fully makes sense when applied to life in general rather than the workplace in particular. This is because some of an individual's needs, particularly the higher ones, may be satisfied outside the workplace. This holistic view is important within the workplace, as employers increasingly recognise that

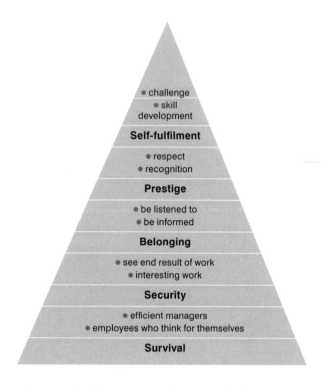

Figure 3: Twyla Dell's mapping of Maslow's hierarchy

individuals' lives outside work impinge on their performance at work.

Although the theory is now over 50 years old, it is still referred to by managers and offers them useful insights. Along with Herzberg and McGregor, Maslow is recognised as one of the founding fathers of motivation theory.

Conducting a performance appraisal

A performance appraisal is a face-to-face discussion between an employee and another person – usually the employee's line manager – in which the employee's performance at work is discussed, reviewed and assessed, using an agreed and understood framework

An effective performance appraisal offers managers the opportunity to gain a deeper understanding of those who report to them and how they work – their achievements, their potential and their development needs. It can also help to motivate and engage employees, improve their performance in their work role, facilitate their personal development and enhance their contribution to organisational objectives. For employees, the performance appraisal should deepen their understanding of their work and what is expected of them, provide recognition of their achievements and give them an opportunity to discuss any problems or development needs they have. It also encourages them to take ownership of, and responsibility for, their performance and personal development.

Priorities, workloads, plans for personal development, and individual and organisational targets and objectives should all be discussed. Feedback on past performance should be given and future goals agreed.

Performance appraisal meetings should not be seen as one-off events; they formalise ongoing performance discussions between employees and their line managers and support the process of performance management in the workplace. In the past it has been common practice for performance appraisals to take place annually, but six-monthly meetings are now much more the norm, often alternating with development-focused reviews and supported with additional, regular meetings to discuss current activities and progress towards objectives.

This checklist aims to help managers prepare for and carry out performance appraisals in a positive and professional manner and gain the maximum benefits from the process.

Action checklist

1 Prepare for the meeting

The difficult part of appraising performance is the preparation prior to the meeting. If your organisation has an established scheme, this will provide a framework for the interview. If not, the following outline structure gives a starting point:

- objectives for the period under review; level of achievement/ progress
- continuing or unresolved problems during this period
- evaluation of any development activity during this period
- objectives for next review period
- support required to achieve these objectives
- personal development objectives – these may vary from the above, or provide a means to their attainment
- any issues of major importance or concern relating to the forthcoming review period.

Gather your thoughts, information and evidence and fit these into the framework. This will help steer the discussion.

2 Arrange for the appraisal discussion

Before the interview, make sure that the appraisee understands the purpose and aims of the appraisal.

- Advise the appraisee how to prepare in advance, for example by identifying strengths, achievements, weaknesses or failures over the past year.

- Ask the appraisee to prepare an assessment of how well the last set of objectives was achieved, and consider what the next year's objectives should be.

- Ask the appraisee to reflect on the value and practical application of any training or development activities undertaken during the past year.

- Explain that this is an opportunity to look at problems, and discuss and agree work directions and methods for the coming year.

- If the appraisal is linked to pay or promotion, explain how this works.

- Introduce any necessary documentation and forms that will be used.

- Agree the time and place for the discussion.

3 Prepare the environment

The environment for the discussion should be informal, friendly, comfortable, and completely private and confidential. Avoid sitting the appraisee in front of your desk, as this could form a barrier; instead, arrange your chairs so that you can communicate easily. Avoid interruptions, and divert or switch off your telephone.

4 Use the consultative approach

It is important to be conversational but positive, discussing specific activities and issues. Focus on looking forward to improvements, ask open questions and listen attentively to what is said. Reflect back what you hear and respond appropriately. Coaching skills will be helpful here.

5 Start the discussion

At the start of the discussion, it is important to relax the appraisee. There is no formula for this, but it is always important to show tact and respect. Gauge the required level of formality and the acceptability of relaxing banter or conversation from how well you know and work with the appraisee.

- Restate the meeting's purpose and structure.
- Emphasise the aim of supporting the appraisee's development.
- Restate the reasons for using documentation (it gives a record of the meeting and its contents, and a base for measuring progress).

6 Develop the discussion

In theory, and with good preparation by both parties, discussion should follow the framework outlined. To try to keep it on track, the appraiser should:

- encourage, but not lead, self-assessment and diagnosis
- maintain and build the appraisee's self-esteem, where appropriate
- offer help and suggestions, but let the appraisee arrive at their own solutions
- concentrate on job performance rather than focus on personalities
- discuss specific examples and not make general comments or criticisms
- summarise the discussions at critical or agreed action points
- give guidance on, and reach agreement about, goals and plans.

7 Deal with difficulties and focus on improvements

If regular conversations and discussions have been taking place, there should be no surprises at this stage. If, however, there is a need to address poor performance, focus on the need for improvement and discuss with the appraisee how and when improvements might be made, and what support might be needed to help achieve them. If appropriate, be prepared to admit that you – as appraiser – might be a cause of problems yourself, or could do more to help the appraisee. If there is disagreement, stay calm but firm. Try to focus on the evidence available and be prepared to consider carefully any counter-evidence presented by the appraisee. Avoid arguing and listen attentively, taking care to separate facts from feelings. Remember that the focus should stay on the job the appraisee does, not on the appraisee personally.

8 Agree areas for improvement

Try to distinguish areas that need remedial attention from those that are developmental. Agree preferred training outcomes and development activities, and encourage the appraisee to identify ways to achieve these. If encouragement is not successful, try steering and guidance, using instruction only as a last resort. Remember that there are many types of training activity, so a standard, public, two-day course is not always the most efficient or appropriate option.

9 Rate the performance

Some appraisal schemes use performance ratings. These can vary in nature and scope and can be useful or destructive, depending on how the rating is done and generally understood. Ratings can be detrimental if they are not:

- fair – reflecting performance against expectations, not other people
- honest – respecting what the individual has to say
- flexible – reflecting the level and extent of individuals' achievements
- consistent – across different sectors of the organisation.

10 Close the discussion

Ensure you have reached and agreed a mutual understanding of the appraisee's objectives, how they will be achieved and the target or review dates. Agree who is doing what to set up these activities and set a date for follow-up. Ensure that you or the employee write up the objectives and plans, preferably on a form used across the organisation, so that both of you can sign it off. End on a positive note.

As a manager you should avoid:

- criticising the appraisee's personality
- basing an assessment of performance over the whole period on a recent incident
- allowing personal prejudice to label the appraisee as good or bad (halo or horns effect)
- using closed, rhetorical questions
- talking rather than listening – a recommended ratio would be 70% listening to 30% talking
- letting the conversation become one-sided
- allowing fear to lead to a good review rather than an truthful one
- ignoring appraisees' views and thoughts
- planning action without first reaching agreement on what is needed.

Undertaking a disciplinary interview

A disciplinary interview is a meeting between at least one manager and an employee (who may be accompanied by a colleague or trade union representative) to investigate and deal with an employee's misconduct or performance in a fair and consistent manner.

Managers often do not find it easy to address issues of poor performance or misconduct, but failing to tackle them can allow problems to escalate and cause further damage to working relationships and organisational performance.

Handling disciplinary issues in a timely, fair and effective manner can:

- identify the causes of poor performance or misconduct and provide solutions to remedy them
- avoid the need for more serious action against an employee later
- aid general morale – although an ineffective process will have the opposite effect.

Ineffective handling of disciplinary issues will:

- leave the employee unclear about the problem or unaware of the need for improvement
- lead to claims of unfair dismissal in some circumstances
- undermine employees' respect for the manager.

This checklist provides guidance for managers who need to carry out a formal interview to address unacceptable behaviour or poor performance, as part of a disciplinary procedure, assuming that it has not been possible to resolve the issue informally.

Action checklist

1 Prepare for the interview

Preparation and planning before the interview are essential in order to be fair and accurate in making a decision. The procedure – and the tone – should be as positive as possible to preserve relationships, help prevent any recurrence of the problem and facilitate improved behaviour.

Gather all the facts

Obtain any written evidence, such as attendance records or production figures that highlight the problem. Aim for a balanced view, taking into account any special circumstances inside or outside work that may help to explain the problem – for example, low staffing levels, increased demand leading to work overload, personal caring responsibilities.

Check the employee's record

Find out about the employee's previous disciplinary history, if any. In the case of performance issues there should be an 'audit trail' showing when the matter has been raised informally or through a performance appraisal. Employees should be made aware of any performance shortcomings and the standards expected of them, and be given time to improve, before formal disciplinary procedures are initiated.

Check the organisation's disciplinary procedure

You should always refer to your HR department to check the policies and procedures in place and the options open to you if the employee is guilty of misconduct, bearing in mind their disciplinary record and the seriousness of the offence. In the UK it is important to ensure that you comply with the ACAS Code of

Practice on Disciplinary and Grievance Procedures, which sets out principles for handling disciplinary and grievance issues fairly. While this is not a statutory procedure, it does represent good practice and UK employment tribunals will expect employers to conform to it.

Look for similar cases and outcomes

Confer with colleagues to see if they have dealt with similar cases and what the outcomes were. Also try to find out whether the employee is committing an offence that is widespread, for example persistent breaking of the dress code or bad timekeeping. Is the employee being singled out unfairly for an offence that should be tackled organisation-wide?

Draw up an outline for the interview

Although no disciplinary interviews will follow exactly the same path, a brief structure should be mapped out. Start by trying to define what you need to achieve from the interview and note important points that need to be covered. Thought should be given to the reasons, mitigating circumstances or excuses that the employee might cite and how these should be recorded for checking later. Consider who should be present at the interview, including witnesses.

2 Inform the employee

The employee should be informed in writing of:

- the reason why they face a disciplinary interview
- the time and place of the interview
- who will be present and who may accompany the employee at the interview.

In the UK employees have a statutory right to be accompanied at all disciplinary hearings by a colleague or a trade union representative. This companion may address the hearing to put the employee's case, sum up the case or respond on the employee's behalf to any view expressed at the hearing. The companion may confer with the employee during the hearing but does not have the right to answer questions on their behalf or address the hearing if the employee does not want them to do so, or to prevent anyone, including the employee, from making a contribution to the hearing.

Determine whether all present should have access to all documents – in some cases this may not be in the employee's best interests.

Remember to give sufficient notice for the employee to prepare their case. The room where the meeting is to be held must be large enough to accommodate those attending comfortably. A phone is useful to call witnesses, but arrange for incoming calls to be diverted to avoid unnecessary interruptions.

It is important for notes to be taken during the meeting to ensure that an accurate record is kept, rather than relying on varying recollections of what was said. The person responsible for taking notes should be informed in advance and witnesses contacted to check their availability. If witnesses cannot be present, obtain written statements from them.

3 Conduct the interview

Disciplinary interviews are stressful for both the manager and the employee. Their ultimate purpose is to create a satisfactory environment for all employees. Remember to try to stay calm and collected; do not allow the interview to develop into a free-for-all shouting match, and ensure that the employee is aware that the interview is part of a formal disciplinary process.

The length of the interview will depend on many factors, but it may become clear at any stage either that the problem has been resolved or that there needs to be further investigation – in this case the proceedings should be adjourned. Similarly, the interview should be called to a halt if matters get heated or become unconstructive. There is no set structure for a disciplinary interview, but here is one approach that may be used.

Introduction

Introduce the people present and the reason for them being there (including a manager or someone from the HR department, acting as a witness and taking notes, and any trade union representative).

Communicate the reason for holding a disciplinary interview. Emphasise that it is part of the organisation's disciplinary procedure, which exists to ensure that all employees are treated equally and fairly.

Tell the employee how the interview will be structured: that is, with the case against them being presented first, followed by the employee's reply.

Present the case against the employee

Detail the case against the employee, including any dates and times that breaches of discipline occurred. If the case has moved some way along the disciplinary procedure, present an outline of the previous stages, the actions taken and the results. In the case of performance issues, it can be helpful to outline what is required to achieve the required standards and highlight reviews, feedback and support that can be offered.

Call on any witnesses to state what they have seen or heard, or knew; alternatively, read out the written statements if witnesses are unable to attend.

Allow the employee to reply

Let the employee respond to the case against them and present evidence, including witnesses and statements. Listen carefully to what the employee has to say, and do not interrupt while they are speaking.

Discuss the case

Allow both sides to ask questions, particularly about ambiguous issues in the evidence. Ask open-ended questions to gain a general picture and more precise questions for specific information. It is important to ascertain whether there were any valid mitigating circumstances, of which you were unaware, for the employee's behaviour. Allow the employee to suggest ways in which the problem can be overcome.

Summarise the case

Following the discussion, the main points from both sides should be reiterated and the whole case summarised. When both sides have agreed this to be correct, the interview should be adjourned so that thought can be given to what action is to be taken or whether further investigation will take place. This will also help allay any suspicions that the outcome was predetermined. However, try to reach a conclusion as quickly as possible to keep anxiety or doubt to a minimum.

4 Inform the employee of the action to be taken

When a decision has been reached, the employee and his/her representative should be brought together and informed of the action to be taken, if any. Actions for improving the situation should be agreed, as appropriate. These may involve the employer as well as the employee. They should be confirmed in writing after the meeting and signed by both parties. In cases concerning performance, it may be appropriate to set a date for review; in cases of misconduct, a further offence will normally trigger the next stage of the formal process, so this should also be confirmed in writing. The employee must be given clear guidance on the appeals procedure to follow if they disagree with the result of the interview or think they have been treated unfairly.

As a manager you should avoid:

- failing to check and comply with the organisation's disciplinary procedure
- assuming guilt before the interview
- finishing the interview without setting clear goals for the future.

David C. McClelland

Motivation theorist and father of the competency movement

Introduction

David McClelland (1917–98) was an eminent psychologist at Harvard University, most famous for his work on what motivates people to achieve and for his development of the notion of competencies.

Life and career

Born in 1917 in Mount Vernon, New York, McClelland graduated with a BA degree from Wesleyan University in 1938, followed by an MA in 1939 from the University of Missouri. In 1941 he gained a PhD in experimental psychology from Yale. He joined the staff of Harvard University in 1956, after gaining some experience in a few teaching posts, and stayed there for the next thirty years. He was also Distinguished Research Professor of Psychology at Boston University from 1987 until his death in 1998.

McClelland was a Fellow of the American Academy of Sciences from 1957 and, during his lifetime, won many research awards. As a Peace Corps consultant, a US Information Agency consultant and a frequent conference speaker, he often travelled the world.

Besides his academic work, McClelland set up a consultancy called McBer with his colleague, David Berlew, in 1963. It was well known in the early competence field, and later as part of the Hay Institute it became known as Hay McBer. A research division of the Hay Group is now called the McClelland Centre, which focuses on research into human behaviour within an organisational context.

During the early years of his career, McClelland's main research interest was achievement motivation, and he not only applied his ideas in this field to the business world, but also saw their much broader relevance. For example, he investigated the connections between achievement motivation and economic development, as well as the links between achievement motivation and physiology. Important works by McClelland include *The Achievement Motive* (with John Atkinson, Russell Clark and Edgar Lowell, 1953), *The Achieving Society* (1961) and *Power: The Inner Experience* (1975).

McClelland's later work focused on competency and its use in recruitment. He developed ways to assess competencies and help companies to match the right people to the right jobs. This work has been of immense importance within management and the corporate world.

Key theories

Three needs theory

McClelland first became well known for his motivation theory. Following studies using the Thematic Apperception Test in the 1940s, he suggested that a person's needs are built up over their lifetime and are shaped by experience. These ideas are set out in his three needs theory, also referred to as the acquired needs theory or the learned needs theory (explained in *Human Motivation*, 1988).

Over and above basic human needs such as food and shelter, McClelland identifies three different kinds of motivational need:

- the need for achievement (n-ach) – a person motivated by this kind of need wants to achieve and attain goals that are challenging but realistic

- the need for power (n-pow) – a person motivated by need for power wants to gain authority, influence and leadership
- the need for affiliation (n-affil) – a person motivated by a need for affiliation seeks to form relationships and to interact with other people, wanting to be well liked and highly regarded.

McClelland proposed that many people are motivated by a mixture of these needs, but some have a strong tendency towards one particular need. The different needs produce different types of workers, so an employee motivated by a need for affiliation, for example, is likely to be a good teamworker.

McClelland was particularly interested in the first type of need (n-ach), and carried out extensive research relating to people motivated by a high need to achieve. He initially believed that these people would be the type most likely to prove good leaders, but, over time, he modified this thinking. Following further study of the types of needs that produce good managers, McClelland concluded that, while a need for achievement is important, a need for power is also a crucial factor in making a good leader who is capable of influencing and inspiring people rather than trying to achieve things alone.

In his seminal work *The Achieving Society* (1961), McClelland discussed the results of an experimental analysis of the link between culture and stories or narratives. Focusing on tales told in societies such as Ancient Greece or Tudor England, the analysis suggested that certain types of thoughts tend to create related types of action. To take one example, thoughts of ambition tend to lead to accomplishment.

McClelland used this study to link his 'three needs' model to economic development, arguing that the profit motive is a naive oversimplification that is best understood in terms of the need for achievement motive, rather than as simple desire for monetary gain. Achievement motivation is likely to produce entrepreneurial behaviour because individuals who are motivated by n-ach are interested in profitability as a measure of their success and competence. Thus countries with a high percentage of people who are motivated by achievement are likely to experience more economic growth.

Competency theory

In the 1970s, McClelland's interest turned to competencies and their relevance for recruitment. 'Competencies' developed out of the methodology used by McClelland and other McBer researchers based on the 'Behavioural Event Interview', during which the characteristics of outstanding and average performers were identified. The real start of the competency movement is generally traced to an article by McClelland, 'Testing for competence rather than intelligence', in *American Psychologist* (1973). He argued against the use of intelligence and psychometric testing in the recruitment process, suggesting that competency in areas relevant to the job is a much better predictor of suitability for a post.

Three important general competencies which McClelland found to be desirable in employees are:

- empathy
- self-discipline
- initiative.

His work suggested that people without these competencies are less likely than others to gain promotion, experience less work satisfaction and are more likely than others to be dismissed. He believed that these competencies were applicable to life in general, not just to the workplace, and that people with these three traits would also prove to be good citizens.

Specific competencies such as flexibility and leadership were also found to be associated with particular jobs. McClelland developed methods of competency mapping to determine the relevant competencies for each job. The behavioural event interview method for determining individual competencies centres upon matching people with appropriate competencies to posts requiring these, and has been widely adopted as a comparatively effective selection and assessment technique.

McClelland also focused on the development of competencies. He believed that, while competencies are to some extent in-built, they can be modified by training. This infers that a poor performer can be encouraged to improve his or her performance through training to develop the required job competencies.

The competency movement gained ground during the 1980s and 1990s. Richard E. Boyatzis gave the first full definition of job competency in *The Competent Manager: Model for Effective Performance* (1982), describing a competency as an underlying individual characteristic causally related to effective or superior performance in a job. Later, a dictionary of competencies developed by McBer researchers was included in a book, *Competence at Work: Models for Superior Performance*, by Lyle M. Spencer and Signe M. Spencer (1993). In this book, based on hundreds of research studies into competencies, the authors delineate twenty-one competencies that are held by superior performers in mid- and upper-level jobs.

In perspective

McClelland's writing on motivation and competencies was groundbreaking, and many others have since built upon it. His three needs theory on motivation is within the tradition of, and has links to, the work of classic theorists such as Frederick Herzberg, Douglas McGregor and Abraham Maslow. Competencies have many practical applications and have been widely researched and discussed, and the use of competency testing is now established as a valued selection and assessment method.

Other models that can be related to McClelland's work include John Adair's action-centred leadership theory and Paul Hersey and Ken Blanchard's situational leadership model.

McClelland's influence has extended into other areas, including sociology, economics, religion and politics. For example, he once entered the political arena to state that the US could better help developing countries by investing in a man, not just in a plan. He saw the need for a person with the right kind of motivational need to implement the plan in order for it to succeed.

The great importance of McClelland's work to organisations is made plain by the speed with which the idea of competency was taken up in practice and the prevalence that it now enjoys. His original approach to research and his highly influential ideas make it hard to underestimate his importance as a management thinker.

Development for passive people

Passive behaviour is generally characterised by a desire to avoid conflict and always please others.

This checklist is intended for line managers leading individuals who are perceived as excessively passive in their behaviour and are failing to make the active contribution you feel they are capable of. Passive people are often pleasant and eager to please, not wanting to face up to difficult situations because they do not wish to upset others. They may be overly compliant, conciliatory or self-effacing. However, this may cover underlying problems or difficulties and may lead them to give in to unrealistic and unachievable demands, saying 'yes' when they need to say 'no', or at least 'but'. They may keep problems to themselves and play it safe to avoid any risks. At worst, they turn into 'yes people' who tell you what they think you want to hear, rather than what they really feel. This means that you will not get a clear picture of the situation in the workplace and will not be able to address issues that need to be dealt with. Eventually, they may lose the confidence of colleagues, including their manager.

Managers should aim to identify the underlying problem and support the individual in their development, encouraging them to make progress towards a more assertive and confident approach and to realise their full potential.

Three key indicators of overly passive behaviour are:

- spoken language – people who behave passively tend to use

words like, 'I'm sorry to bother you, but', or 'I know I'm probably wrong, but'

- body language – telltale signs of passive behaviour include:
  - an inability to make eye contact
  - stooping and keeping their head down
  - nervous gestures, like fingering their collar or playing with a pencil
  - speaking abnormally quietly
  - using an excessive amount of 'ums' and 'ers'

- work results – passive people tend not to want to disappoint or upset people, so they may take on too much work, get overloaded and then struggle to keep up.

Passive people often confuse assertive behaviour with aggressive behaviour and find it difficult to act assertively. They think that if they make a firm statement they are being aggressive, and they equate passive behaviour with politeness. The advantages of developing more assertive behaviour can include:

- gaining confidence – their self-esteem rises and this reinforces the new behaviour

- being less prone to missing deadlines, improving communication and airing problems, thus reducing the potential for conflict

- learning, with encouragement, to take responsibility for their own decisions and to solve problems that they previously referred upwards or sideways

- achieving better results and causing fewer problems.

Action checklist

1 Understand passive behaviour

The first step in dealing with passivity is to understand some of the possible reasons people behave this way. Their behaviour may reflect their natural personality; it may be a conscious choice; or it may be the result of bad experiences, trauma in the past or difficult circumstances in the present. Additional factors may include:

- the mistaken belief that they will be disliked if they disagree and that others always like someone who agrees with them
- the desire to please, sacrificing long-term reality for short-term compliance and agreement
- the feeling that other people are threatening or intimidating
- failing to understand that they have the right to their own views and ideas
- not having confidence in their own views and ideas
- being fearful of disapproval and of getting things wrong
- lack of awareness of assertiveness techniques, and an inability to see themselves as others do.

2 Consider the working environment

The working environment has a strong influence on personal behaviour. So don't simply blame the individual for their passivity, but consider whether organisational factors are involved. Is this an isolated case, or is there any evidence that it is more widespread? Analyse the culture of the organisation: does it encourage individuals to express their views openly and behave assertively and creatively? If possible, consider what you can learn from how the individual behaved during their interview and their socialisation on joining the organisation. Has there been a misunderstanding linked with the behaviour now being perceived as negative? Were there misunderstandings in those early encounters that have influenced how they think they ought to behave? These are the types of questions you need to ask as you engage in clear communication with the individual.

3 Analyse the dynamics of your team

Analyse your team's dynamic and the personalities within it. Do they make it easy for the more introverted individuals to offer opinions, or is a set of dominant views simply accepted by all as being right? The make-up of your team could well be reinforcing passive behaviour. If so, attempt to counterbalance more dominant personalities with submissive ones by actively engaging passive individuals, encouraging them to contribute and socialise with the rest of the group. Ask their opinion, in a team meeting for example, to foster social interaction. However, refrain from singling them out, as this may make them feel 'exposed' and unwilling to participate voluntarily in future discussions. Aim to create an environment that encourages participation and interaction, and allows them to speak openly and honestly.

4 Take account of cultural differences

Be aware of cultural differences and ask yourself whether you are judging an individual based on your own cultural perspective. Are the dominant cultural norms in the group making it difficult for an individual to perform well? An individual's beliefs, the way in which they live and were raised, have a strong influence on how they behave in the workplace. Such differences should be recognised and respected, and you will need to work out how best to adapt working practices to accommodate and take advantage of them.

5 Demonstrate tact and diplomacy

A sensitive approach to communication is necessary to gain an understanding as to the possible reasons for passive behaviour. Allocate time to ask questions and, more importantly, to listen. Conduct such conversations somewhere private to ensure confidentiality. It is important to realise that for most passive people their attitudes and behaviour are deeply ingrained. They are not something that can be changed overnight. Simply telling a passive person to 'assert themselves more' can make the situation worse. Be sensitive to the individual's values, preferences and feelings and be mindful of their self-esteem. Be clear what your expectations of them are so as to avoid any misunderstanding.

6 Act as a role model

Show how effective assertive behaviour can be by demonstrating it yourself. If passive staff members can see that their manager acts assertively, listens to problems and finds constructive solutions without apportioning blame, they are more likely to be encouraged to act the same way themselves. Focus the spotlight upon yourself: are you a good role model in encouraging assertiveness? Are the ways in which you are approaching the relationship encouraging the perceived passive behaviour? Be honest with yourself, as you may well find that you are inadvertently adding to this passivity. Remember that as the team leader you are under scrutiny. How you deal with individuals will be observed by others, potentially leading to misunderstandings or unintended consequences.

7 Seek guidance from others

Get a second opinion by consulting colleagues, particularly those with whom the individual comes into regular contact. Check your assessment against theirs and seek advice before taking an initiative that could damage relationships. You may find that others don't agree with your perception of an individual's passive nature. What one person sees as negative may be viewed by another as positive. One person's 'passivity' is another's 'quiet efficiency'. However, if it becomes apparent that there is indeed a recognised behavioural issue affecting the employee's performance, consider involving a specialist rather than risk doing something that could harm the organisation, your team and the individual.

8 Find ways to address the situation

If an organisational performance management system is in place, it may be appropriate to address the issue in that context, through performance appraisal interviews or development reviews. However, bear in mind that management and/or training alone may not alter how people act or behave, and individuals may be unable, or unwilling, to shrug off their socialisation and value sets. Nonetheless, a carefully considered approach may prove beneficial, helping individuals to take responsibility for their personal development and encouraging them to realise their potential.

Informal coaching or one-on-one mentoring may be helpful. However, if there is a serious behavioural issue affecting individual performance specialist help may be required.

Encourage assertiveness by:

- fostering an open environment where people feel supported and are able to speak freely

- coaching individuals in techniques and approaches to achieve assertiveness

- providing opportunities to increase confidence – for example, a situation where the passive person can try out new skills and be assured of success

- giving regular feedback on performance and behaviour, making sure to recognise good performance. Positive reinforcement is a powerful tool for changing how people think and act.

As a manager you should avoid:

- blaming the individual for their passivity

- being irritated and unsympathetic about the situation

- ignoring the situation and hoping it will go away

- failing to take cultural differences into account

- taking decisive action based upon personal assessment of the individual without consulting with peers and colleagues first.

Motivating the demotivated

Motivation is defined as the needs, drives and desires that direct human actions and thoughts. Those needs range from physical (food, shelter) to emotional (need to belong, recognition, love) to cognitive (making sense of the world), and their intensity and scope influence behaviour and perception of the environment in every human being.

A growing body of research evidence supports the common-sense view that employees who are engaged with their work and keen to do it to the best of their ability are more likely to produce good results than those who are bored and disinterested. Demotivated employees can also exert a negative influence on other employees, with repercussions for morale in the team, department and ultimately the organisation as a whole. This checklist offers advice for managers who feel that a team member appears demotivated and who wish to improve levels of energy, commitment and morale. There are many reasons, but some would argue that people are not unmotivated; it's just that the right motivational triggers have not yet been found. Important keys to improving motivation are to identify the cause, to gain an understanding of what makes people tick and to do what you can to address the issue.

Action checklist

1 Find out what does motivate them

The better you know your colleagues/employees the better you can manage them. So get to know them. This doesn't necessarily mean sharing evenings out or chatting about what happened at the weekend. It does involve trying to form an objective view of what matters to them – what drives each individual. You may have been trying the wrong things.

Try asking: 'What's important to you in your work?', 'What annoys you?', 'Has anything changed lately?'

Listen and note down the responses. Typical examples include:

- **Being appreciated for what I do and feeling that I have achieved something.** In this case, try to find out what kind of appreciation they have in mind, for example promotion, bonus, public praise and recognition, private recognition, more responsibility, new tasks, job security.

- **Doing a good job and enjoying myself.** Find out what they mean by enjoyment, for example working with people they like, completing projects on time, not working too hard.

- **Solving problems and making sure things don't go wrong.** Does this come from being the expert, motivating others to get things right, managing and organising, or solving problems as a team? Which stage of problem-solving do they enjoy most, for example developing new ideas and concepts, implementing plans, organising and supervising?

Once you are clear about this, you will be able to reframe their work in terms of what it is that motivates them. It is important to remember that what is motivating for some may well be demotivating for others.

2 Reflect their own words

Once you have identified what's important to the other person about their work, take the words they have used and show how they can be motivated in their work. Let's look at each example in detail.

- **Being appreciated for what I do and feeling that I have achieved something.** This person needs you to tell them how much you appreciate what they do. You also need to talk to them in terms of what they are going to achieve – not what you want them to do. For example: 'We need to sell 5,000 of these by the end of the year. How can we achieve that?' rather than 'You must work harder to sell more of these.'

- **Doing a good job and enjoying myself.** In this case you probably need to ask what they mean by doing a good job. Most people think they know, but it's different for different people. Once you know this, you can help them. For example, it might be:
  - 'finishing what I started at the beginning of the day'
  - 'having satisfied customers'
  - 'doing the job to the best of my ability'.

  You also need to find out what they enjoy, so that you can help them to enjoy their work.

- **Solving problems and making sure things don't go wrong.** This is someone who likes solving problems, so you need to talk about work issues as problems and use that language when you speak to them. They may well not be motivated by goals and targets, but will be delighted if you tell them you have a really difficult problem to solve and no one else can fix it. Sometimes one individual's negativity is another's positivity. By using reverse psychology and informing someone of what could go wrong, you can motivate them to do a better job.

3 Treat all your team members as individuals

All these matters are highly personal. Your approach won't be the same for any two people. So find out exactly what an individual wants and what you can do to help them. In the examples given in the second bullet point above, for example, you need to:

- ask the individual what will enable them to finish what they started at the beginning of the day and how you can help them to achieve this goal

- find out who the individual thinks the customers are and then how they can be satisfied – it may be that the customers are already satisfied but the individual is not aware of this

- find out what the individual means by the 'best of my ability' and how that can be measured.

Think about your employees as a team and what motivates them as a team, as opposed to other teams. What incentives can you set on the team level to increase team cohesion and performance? Individual and team motivation need to go together. Which level you choose to address will depend on your analysis of the current situation, the tasks at hand and the goals you need to achieve.

Team motivation can work as a strategy for integrating 'difficult' individuals. As a rule, people do not want to be left out or to stand out too much. So if you can find incentives that motivate all the team except one, that one employee is likely to make at least some effort.

4 Have clear goals

Psychologically, it is unlikely that whatever goals the demotivated individuals have, they are not supporting work performance. For managers it is always best to work from the position that everyone has goals, but they might not be those that are needed at work. It is uncommon for people to have no goals. It is more likely that there is a lack of clarity about goals, or that different managers or supervisors have set conflicting goals, for example, for employees who participate in a number of teams within the organisation. Check for goal incongruence.

It is possible, however, that no goals have been set or that individuals are unable to set goals themselves. Finding it hard to set goals can be a consequence of stress. It can also happen when individuals set themselves goals, or have had goals set for them, which are just so big and overwhelming that they struggle to identify the steps that will help them to work towards them.

5 Offer help with planning

Similarly, once the goals are clear, it can be helpful to work with individuals to identify a series of steps that will help them to achieve their objectives. This can be handled by asking them what they need to do. If they come up with large or daunting tasks, again, help them to break the larger steps down into smaller, manageable ones. Bear in mind, though, that some employees will be better motivated if they are allowed do all the planning themselves; in such cases it is better not to interfere with the way they achieve their goals.

6 Take time to explain

It is also possible that it is a question not of being unmotivated but of being uninformed. Some leaders may operate under the illusion that because they are familiar with the organisation's goals and targets, all their team members are as well. Usually, this is not the case. Having clear goals is one thing; making sure that they are effectively communicated and understood may be quite another.

Take time to explain team or departmental and organisational goals, and make sure that everyone has understood and assimilated their role and the contribution they need to make towards achieving these goals. Knowing the reasons behind a particular objective can often be helpful in making choices in the course of the working day.

Identifying personal drivers and incentives also means that, whenever possible, you can allocate responsibilities to a team member which lie within their areas of interest. Linking personal goals and contributions to the organisation's objectives is a double win.

7 Involve the unmotivated in coming up with solutions

You may well ask an unmotivated person what it is they want or need; they may well tell you what it is they don't want. Negativity may arise from a number of sources, but you should try to follow up on negative remarks by finding out what they really want.

- Answer: 'I do not want to work on this project.'
- Question: 'What sort of project do you want to work on?'
- Answer: 'One that's not like this.'
- Question: 'Would you like more responsibility, independence, resources, scope, people, etc?'
- Answer: 'More independence.'

8 Try to get buy-in

If people make a personal decision to attempt something, they are generally far more likely to be motivated to achieve it than if a task is imposed upon them or they are instructed to do a particular job. Involvement generates buy-in and ownership. Conversely, if people's views and ideas are not reflected in the way forward, they may feel that no one is listening to them, or that solutions are being generated that do not make use of everybody's contribution and experience. Either way, demotivation can set in.

9 Make sure the rules are clear

Have you ever embarked on a project only to find that the goal posts have shifted? Weeks into the project you are told that you need to change what you are doing because some ground rule, or constraint, or working method was not made clear. Clear briefing on the rules of procedure is as important as the clear communication of goals.

10 Be negative yourself

People who appear demotivated can often be motivated more by problems or things that might go wrong than by goals. If you are the kind of person who talks exclusively about goals and targets, they may not relate to what you say. It's not that they don't care, it's more that this just doesn't press their buttons. One of the most strange but effective techniques to use with people like this is to tell them that things are really difficult or impossible. This may seem odd to you, but to them it can be really motivating.

It is important to bear in mind that people with high self-esteem and high perceived self-efficacy are motivated by problems and negative feedback. Because they are resourceful, they see it not as criticism but as a challenge, and it will increase their motivation to succeed. People with low self-esteem and low self-efficacy, however, can become even more demotivated by negative feedback. They need positive goals to look forward to.

So different treatment is needed for different employees. If you are working with people of the former kind, tell them what will go wrong if they don't do something, or describe the problems you need to solve rather than talking about targets.

11　Consider alternative action

Having tried the above and probably some other strategies too, it may be that you are dealing with someone who is deliberately negative, or is awkward for the sake of it. Such people might not respond to any triggers, thereby having a demoralising and detrimental impact on the whole team. These people may well find that another working environment is more suited to them. In such cases, it may be appropriate to suggest that they move on for their own benefit as well as that of the team.

As a manager you should avoid:

- allowing demotivated employees to damage team morale and performance
- making assumptions about what motivates individuals
- thinking that the same approach will work with everyone.

Frederick Herzberg
The hygiene-motivation theory

Introduction

Frederick Herzberg (1923–2000) was an American clinical psychologist who later became Professor of Management at Utah University. His 'overriding interest in mental health' stemmed from his belief that 'mental health is the core issue of our times'. This was prompted by his posting to the Dachau concentration camp after its liberation. On his return to the US, he worked for the Public Health Service.

His hygiene-motivation theory was first published in *The Motivation to Work* in 1959. Herzberg's work focused on the individual in the workplace, but it has been popular with managers as it also emphasises the importance of management knowledge and expertise.

The hygiene-motivation theory

The 'hygiene-motivation' or 'two-factor' theory resulted from research with 200 Pittsburgh engineers and accountants, who were asked what pleased and displeased them about their jobs. From their responses, Herzberg concluded that human beings have two sets of needs:

- lower-level needs as an animal to avoid pain and deprivation
- higher-level needs as a human being to grow psychologically.

Some factors in the workplace meet the first set of needs but not the second and vice versa. The first group he called 'hygiene factors' and the second 'motivators'.

Herzberg also coined the term 'job enrichment', a technique that grew out of the hygiene-motivation theory. Job enrichment involved including motivators in the design of jobs. In a famous *Harvard Business Review* article, 'One more time: how do you motivate employees?', published in 1968, Herzberg also invented the acronym KITA (Kick In The Ass) to explain personnel practices such as wage increases, fringe benefits and job participation that were developed as attempts to instil motivation but are only short-term solutions.

Herzberg used KITA to explain why managers don't motivate employees. He demonstrated that employees are not motivated by being kicked (figuratively speaking), or by being given more money or benefits, a comfortable environment or reducing time spent at work. He called these elements hygiene factors because they concern the context or environment in which a person works.

Hygiene factors also include:

- company policy and administration
- supervision
- working relationships
- status and security.

These factors do not in themselves promote job satisfaction, but serve primarily to prevent job dissatisfaction, just as good hygiene does not in itself produce good health, but a lack of it will cause disease. Herzberg also speaks of them as dissatisfiers or maintenance factors, since it is their absence or inadequacy that causes dissatisfaction at work. Some factors are not true motivators, as they need constant reinforcement. Additionally, they increasingly come to be regarded as rights to be expected, rather than incentives to greater satisfaction and achievement.

Motivators (also referred to as growth factors) relate to what a person does at work, rather than the context in which it is done. They include:

- achievement
- recognition
- the work itself
- responsibility
- advancement and growth.

Herzberg explains that the two sets of factors are separate and distinct because they are concerned with two different sets of needs. They are not opposites.

Herzberg's hygiene-motivation theory is derived from the outcomes of several investigations into job satisfaction and job dissatisfaction, studies that replicated his original research in Pittsburgh. The theory proposes that most factors contributing to job satisfaction are motivators (achievement, recognition, the satisfaction of the work itself, responsibility, and opportunities for advancement and growth) and most factors contributing to job dissatisfaction are hygiene elements (company policy, general management, individuals' relationship with their manager and working conditions).

Most of the evidence on which Herzberg based his theory is relatively clear. This is particularly the case with regard to achievement and promotion prospects as potential job satisfiers, and supervision and job insecurity as contributors principally to dissatisfaction.

The element that continues to stimulate debate is salary/pay, which seems split down the middle. Herzberg's evidence was not so clear here, although he placed salary with the dissatisfiers. This would seem to be the most appropriate classification; although pay may have some short-term motivational value, it is difficult to conceive of it as a long-term motivator in the same way as responsibility and achievement. Most experience (and the history of industrial relations) would point to pay as a dissatisfier and therefore a hygiene factor along with supervision, status and security.

Herzberg used biblical allusions to illustrate his theory. He depicted human beings' basic needs as two parallel arrows pointing in opposite directions. One arrow shows their Animal-Adam nature, concerned with the need to avoid physical deprivation (the hygiene factors), the other their Human-Abraham nature, needing to realise the potential for perfection (the motivation factors).

Job enrichment was an extension of Herzberg's hygiene-motivation theory. He saw it as a continuous management function that involved embracing motivators in job design. These included:

- self-scheduling
- control of resources
- accountability
- undertaking specialised tasks to become expert in them.

In perspective

Herzberg's ideas have proved extremely durable. A late 1990s article, for example, draws on his classic 1968 *Harvard Business Review* article, and adapts his 'hygiene' and 'satisfier' factors to apply them to customer satisfaction (Earl Naumann and Donald W. Jackson, 'One more time – how do you satisfy customers?', *Business Horizons*, vol. 42, no. 3, May/June 1999, pp. 71–6). His work can be seen – in common with that of Elton Mayo (known for the Hawthorne experiments), Abraham Maslow (developer of the hierarchy of needs) and Douglas McGregor (creator of theory X and theory Y) – as a reaction to F. W. Taylor's scientific management theories. These focused on techniques that could be used to maximise the productivity of manual workers and on the separation of mental and physical work between management and workers. In contrast, Herzberg and his contemporaries believed that workers wanted the opportunity to feel part of a team and to grow and develop.

Although Herzberg's theory is not highly regarded by psychologists today, managers have found in it useful guidelines for action. Its basic tenets are easy to understand and can be applied to all types of organisation. Furthermore, it appears to support the position and influence of management.

More specifically, its impact has been seen on reward systems, first in a move away from payment-by-results systems and today in the growing proportion of cafeteria benefits schemes, which allow individual employees to choose the fringe benefits that best suit them.

Job enrichment was more theorised about than put into practice. Many schemes that were tried resulted only in cosmetic changes or led to demands for increased worker control and were therefore terminated. Nowadays the concept is more one of people enrichment, although this still owes much to Herzberg's original work. His greatest contribution has been the knowledge that motivation comes from within the individual; it cannot be imposed by an organisation according to some formula. Many of today's trends – career management, self-managed learning and empowerment – have a basis in Herzberg's insights.

Managing the plateaued performer

'A performance plateau is a levelling off of growth during which productivity flattens out and results remain stagnant.' (Theodore Kurtz)

A performer who has reached a certain level in the company and appears to be 'stuck' – to have neither the ambition nor the ability, or indeed the opportunity, to progress further – has reached a plateau. There may be nothing wrong with their present performance, but they have no new ideas or initiatives and provide no inspiration to their own staff.

A person shouldn't be categorised as having reached a plateau until their performance has remained static for at least one year, maybe even two. The person is also likely to have been in the same job, or the same department, for some time.

This checklist is concerned with the handling of employees who have apparently reached a plateau in their performance and still have some years to serve. It is aimed at managers who are immediately responsible for these employees.

An employee reaching a plateau in their performance is a common phenomenon, especially in flat organisations where there is less chance of promotion. It may be tempting to ignore the issue, as it poses no immediate threat. However, boredom and staleness can easily be the result for the employee, if they simply carry on doing their job in a routine way. If not tackled, their performance may decline, to the disadvantage of the organisation and themselves.

Effective management of the performer who has reached a plateau should ensure, at the very least, that the person continues to make a significant contribution to the organisation, and at best makes new contributions.

The experience of such people can be valuable as long as they maintain good performance levels. The manager should get to know the person and try to identify what is holding them back. Indeed, it may not be the fault of the individual but rather something in the organisation that is stopping them going any further, notably at times of pay restraint and in flatter organisational structures. Whatever the reason for the plateau, it is important to start from the premise that something can be done to help. Continued support should be provided, exploring all possible ways of improvement, and likely solutions implemented.

Remember throughout not to treat the person as a problem. Your aim is to see whether and how they can rise off the plateau. Conversely, if they do not want the responsibilities of the next level and are content to maintain their current status, help them to continue their performance to ensure that they are still making a valuable contribution.

Action checklist

1 Try to spot the signs

Reaching a plateau is an emerging process; it doesn't happen overnight. No single incident will present itself as a benchmark or even a diagnosis. Be careful not to confuse plateauing with the Peter Principle. The latter is concerned with employees rising to their level of incompetence. Stable performers, however, cannot channel their energies or abilities into productive performance.

Ask yourself whether the person's productivity has declined consistently or sporadically. Has there been a slackening in interest and commitment? Has their behaviour changed from the norm?

2 **Identify which of the four plateau Ps apply to the individual**

Beverly Kaye has described four different types of plateau:

- Passive – defined by low individual activity, trapped in personal inaction, with the apparent collusion of the employing organisation.

- Productive – the opposite of passive where high activity is the order of the day but 'busyness' does not necessarily equate to effectiveness.

- Partial – there is an absence of promotional or challenging prospects but individuals have their own enthusiasm for work with often one small area of interest or responsibility keeping the personal spark alive.

- Pleasant – happy with their current lot, doing the job well, in a comfortable groove, but wanting no challenges, no risks and with no wish to develop or improve, for example not wanting the stress of a more senior position.

The attitude and level of activity of the individual will help identify which type of plateau you are dealing with.

3 **Get to know the person properly**

Try to understand what makes the person tick, what their interests are, whether there are personal reasons for them remaining on a plateau, whether they are actually content to stay where they are, or whether, for example, earlier failure to get promotion had a demotivating effect. Find out what their ambitions are, both personal and professional.

4 **Examine your relationship with the person and their relationship with the employing organisation**

It may be that there is something in your relationship that is holding the person back. It can be difficult to find out whether this is the case. It may be possible to ask the person directly – they may appreciate you talking to them in an understanding way. It is often necessary, however, to consult colleagues at your own level or above.

5 Identify the problem as precisely as you can

There may be various reasons why an employee has reached a plateau. For example:

- you may not have provided a stimulating environment
- they may feel that you have written them off
- they may have been given no new challenge for a long time
- they may be working with colleagues who largely ignore them
- there may be issues in their personal or home life.

There are many other possible causes, but a lack of stimulus is likely to figure among them.

6 Explore how you can improve matters

Start with a positive assumption that improvement is possible, as this is almost always the case. If you assume that you are unlikely to be able to help but might as well have a go, this attitude is bound to communicate itself to the other person. The solution will usually include providing a new stimulus – few people at any level do not respond to the right stimulus. This might mean no more than making their present job more interesting, pointing out how they could make more of it, giving them a new challenge within their present responsibilities, or working with a team on a special project. It might mean suggesting a change of job within the company.

7 Continue to show interest and give support

At the same time, you should emphasise that the individual must take responsibility for their own future, and make it clear that you will give your support, whatever they decide. A person may make a short-term improvement and then sink back again. Take a continuing interest in the individual, and make it clear that you are doing so without being too obtrusive.

8 Incorporate support for plateaued employees into organisational policy

It is not sufficient to support just one person in your team, and it could even appear that you are singling out individuals for special treatment. As appropriate, bring this issue to the attention of senior management, with a view to providing support for employees who have reached a plateau as part of organisational policy. This will involve all managers in identifying plateaued performers at an early stage and learning how to offer help and support. This will represent the organisation's concern for its main resource: its people. Bear in mind, also, that success with one or two employees can send positive signals to others. However, don't assume that the only way is up. People's motivation will vary and some may be happy as they are. A potential difficulty with pushing people above the plateau is that they may expect some form of recognition and/or reward for their increased efforts. This may not be easy to resolve, and it is the responsibility of the manager to consider what is required to simply stand still against what is needed to progress.

9 Recognise that some employees will stay on a plateau

Although it is always worth doing what you can to develop employees who have reached a plateau, and you will achieve some surprising successes, you won't succeed every time. If you can't raise the sights of an individual after several attempts, you may allow them to continue as they are as long as they are continuing to make a valuable contribution to the organisation. However, if their performance becomes unsatisfactory, appropriate action will need to be taken.

As a manager you should avoid:

- starting with negative assumptions
- being too obstructive
- giving up too easily
- assuming that people want to advance beyond their plateau.

Motivating your employees in a time of change

Motivation is the creation of incentives and working environments that enable people to perform to the best of their ability. The aim of motivation is to engage people with the work they are doing in order to achieve the best possible outcomes for individuals and the organisation as a whole.

In today's constantly changing and competitive environment, it is crucial for organisations to engage and motivate their employees. Those who are motivated and engaged use their talents and abilities to the full and make the best contribution they can to the work of the organisation. Failure to do this can result in a loss of competitiveness and profits.

In spite of the many theories and practical examples available, motivation is still often viewed as difficult to handle. Financial rewards are often perceived as a generic cure to motivation, but this fails to take account of the fact that different individuals are motivated by different things and in different ways. The reality is that monetary rewards work well for tasks that are specific and measurable, but are less successful when creativity and the ability to 'think outside the box' are required. Indeed, at times this approach can even be counterproductive.

Maintaining motivation is particularly important and challenging at times of rapid change and economic uncertainty. Morale can sink dramatically as a result of the insecurity that change can bring, particularly during organisational restructuring or downsizing. It may also be difficult to motivate employees who are on short-term contracts or working as temps. This checklist is designed to help managers engage, motivate and develop employees more effectively in the context of change.

Action checklist

1 Find out more about motivational practice and theory

To gain ideas on motivating people, you could begin by looking at examples of good practice from other companies. You might identify these via the media, through hearsay, or by reading management books and journals.

Classic theories of motivation include Frederick Herzberg's hygiene theory, Douglas McGregor's theory X and theory Y, William Ouchi's theory Z, which he argued achieves a balance between theories X and Y, and Abraham Maslow's hierarchy of needs. These are all still popular, although they date back some years. They differ in nature, but they all see change and motivation as a process. Contemporary thinking in this field includes David MacLeod and Nita Clarke's report, *Engaging for Success*. Looking at theories and real-life examples should stimulate your thoughts, and give you some 'starter' ideas on how to motivate your own people.

2 What motivates you?

Think about the factors in your working life that have been important to you. What has motivated or demotivated you in the past? What motivates your family and friends? Money can be a strong motivator for some. But everyone is different, and for many powerful motivators may include real responsibility, positive support when things go wrong, a need for meaning, status or influence, a sense of belonging, self-development, and working for an organisation whose work they consider valuable or important. Bear in mind that different cultures have different views of motivation and that culture plays an important role in understanding what motivates people.

Understand the difference between real, longer-term motivators and shorter-term spurs such as a new computer or improved canteen facilities.

3 Find out what people want most from their jobs.

People may want higher status, higher pay, better working conditions and a choice of fringe benefits. Find out what their main motives are by asking what they want most from themselves and from the job. You might do this through performance appraisals, employee surveys or informal discussions. Answers people give may include:

- more interesting work
- to work for effective bosses
- to see the end result of their work
- more participation
- greater recognition
- more involvement and challenge
- more opportunities for development
- more responsibility and empowerment.

Remember that clear two-way communication is essential during times of change to ensure employees remain motivated. Find out what motivates each individual and set about addressing it.

4 Walk the job

Every day, find someone who is doing something well and tell them they are doing so. Make sure your interest is genuine, but don't go overboard or appear to watch over people's shoulders. If you have ideas about work improvements, don't shout them out. Instead, help people find their own ways to improve their work. You don't need to be able to do everything better than your team – in fact the contrary is likely to be the case. But set a good example, and make it clear what levels of support you will give to others. The visibility and trust of senior managers is crucial, especially in times of change.

5 Remove demotivators

Identify factors that demotivate staff. These may be psychological (boredom, unfairness, barriers to promotion, lack of recognition, lack of confidence in the company or senior management) or physical (buildings, equipment, noise levels). Some factors can be dealt with easily; others will require more planning and time to work through. Demonstrating your concern to find out what is wrong, and do something about it, should in itself help to boost general morale. Refrain from keeping people in the dark about what is happening – this can instantly demotivate employees, who will feel insecure about or unprepared for the changes afoot. It is also important to recognise and manage any individuals who are having a negative influence on other team members.

6 Demonstrate support

Your working culture may be a demanding one where errors are not tolerated, or a more tolerant one where mistakes are treated as learning opportunities or pointers for development. Either way, people need to know what kind and level of support they can expect from you. Is there any flexibility around the existing rules and procedures? Is it acceptable for them to use their initiative when circumstances indicate a need to adapt the rules? Management support is a hurdle at which motivational practice, and the relationships built around it, can falter. Empower people but be clear in setting boundaries that people can work within, and be sure that they have your full support for as long as they operate within the limits set.

7 Be wary of using only cash incentives

A fair and robust reward system is important in developing a committed workforce, but research suggests that money is often quite low on the list of motivators. Fringe benefits can be effective in attracting new employees but rarely motivate them to use their potential more effectively. Managers' skill in supporting, guiding and relating to members of their team, however, is repeatedly found to be a central factor in employee engagement.

8 Decide on action

Having talked and listened to people, take steps to change existing policies and attitudes in line with your investigatory findings and introduce new ideas on how to improve motivation and morale. Your plans may include new policies on internal promotion, more flexible working hours, increased empowerment, and employee involvement and participation. You may also consider non-monetary incentives, such as recognition or award schemes, vouchers, paid time to serve the local community, discounted goods, or tickets to the theatre or other events. A selection (or flexible variation) of fringe incentives that could be used might include training and development, healthcare benefits, childcare assistance, low-interest loans, help with travel or transport, sabbaticals, or special leave concessions such as study leave. Ask people what they would appreciate in order to identify the most effective means of encouraging motivation and engagement. Whatever policies you consider, it is imperative to ensure that you discuss them fully with employees and trade unions.

For junior or even middle managers, the implementation of such policies may be beyond your remit. In such cases, learn how to influence your senior management to make policy changes.

9 Manage change

To implement the new policies successfully, good communications are essential. Many people have an instinctive resistance to changes that are imposed upon them by others, so encourage employees to be involved in, and contribute to, the planned changes and their implementation. Most of the time, resistance to change is caused by people not understanding the reasons for it, so address this issue. Communicate as much as you can and as often as possible about what is going on and why. Seek people's input at different stages as new policies are set up, and adapt or change the policies in line with feedback people give. Ensure that everyone is able to air their feelings and opinions honestly, so that any widespread problems or issues are immediately clear.

Try to focus on reaching agreement, seeking where possible to win people's involvement and ownership. Also provide timely information and give employees the opportunity to say how change should be managed.

10 Provide feedback

Feedback is a valuable part of the motivation cycle, so let employees know how their development, progress and accomplishments are shaping up. Offer thoughtful comments, and discuss their next steps or future targets. Organisational performance is ultimately driven by the engagement of individuals, so appraisal and development management provide ideal opportunities to develop motivational skills. Create opportunities to give feedback reasonably often, reinforcing the organisation's strategy and culture. Remember that, as a manager, you are the key motivating or demotivating factor for people in your team; the team atmosphere you create and the relationships you build will be a main route to earning people's discretionary effort and cooperation. Providing feedback and seeking employees' opinions are important for keeping them motivated and engaged.

As a manager you should avoid:

- making assumptions about what drives others
- poor communication
- forcing people into things that (you think) will be 'good for them'
- forgetting about the need for inspiration and excitement in the workplace.

Coaching for improved performance

Coaching is a method of helping people develop their skills and knowledge through a one-to-one relationship with a coach (often a more senior or experienced colleague), who provides guidance and support through a range of work-based activities. The coach works with the learner to identify where they could develop new skills, either for their current job or for the future, and provides support and encouragement to help them in achieving their aims. Coaching is essentially non-directive, with the emphasis on helping people to learn, rather than teaching them, and on allowing them to try things out for themselves.

Coaching differs from mentoring in that it deals with specific tasks and skills that can be mastered and measured; mentoring focuses on longer-term development or progress within an organisation. A further distinction between coaching and mentoring is that coaching is almost always a line management function, whereas mentoring is almost always out of the line.

Coaches need excellent interpersonal skills, including:

- a caring, patient and supportive approach
- an awareness of their own strengths and weaknesses
- good verbal and non-verbal communication
- good listening and questioning skills
- the ability to observe and make accurate assessments.

Coaching has attracted much attention in recent years as a method of developing senior leaders and executives. It is also a popular tool for developing employee potential and work performance.

When used appropriately, coaching can be a cost-effective approach to development, focusing on specific individuals and their identified development needs. The need to recruit new employees can be reduced by developing the skills of existing employees. Coaching can also improve motivation, leading to a reduction in staff turnover. It sends a positive message to employees that the organisation values its staff, and creates a sense of achievement for both those acting as coaches and those receiving support from a coach.

Coaching is most effective when used as one of a range of learning and training activities. It can be a good way to reinforce learning and help employees apply theoretical knowledge-based learning acquired from formal training. It may be carried out by external, professional coaches or by internal coaches, who might be line managers, colleagues, or members of the HR department. This checklist is designed for internal coaches, and provides guidance on conducting a coaching session.

It is important to remember that coaching involves one-to-one relationships which require considerable time and effort. Those providing coaching will themselves need training, supervision and support.

Action checklist

1 Gain support and recognition from the organisation

First, gain the support of senior management to ensure that all coaching activity is recognised as being an important part of the working day. Acknowledgment of additional time and resources is essential if the coaching activity is to be a success. If coaches feel that an organisation does not believe such work is a priority compared with other tasks, they may then postpone, cut short or fail to apply maximum effort and concentration during the coaching sessions. This is turn can give learners the negative feeling that they are a low priority in relation to other work. Coaching has a far better chance of success if coaches feel motivated and focused on the task at hand, and that their performance is being monitored, and supported, by their superiors.

2 Plan your approach before starting the session

Hold a preliminary meeting with the learner to establish ground rules:

- identify the learning needs that the coaching sessions will aim to address, and agree on priorities

- set learning objectives – these should be clearly set out (for example, 'By X date you will be able to explain/demonstrate how to do Y')

- agree and define success criteria, or task objectives, between the coach and the learner, specifying the standard against which success will be judged

- review the options and make a detailed plan

- decide on the practicalities – the number and length of sessions to be carried out, location and preferred times of day

- ensure the person wants, or at least understands the need, to be coached, for example for performance reasons.

3 Establish the most appropriate approach to learning

We all learn in different ways. For coaching to be effective, it is essential to understand what will best meet the needs of the learner. Explore and test a mixture of methods, including watching, listening, thinking, reading, observing, reflecting or trying things out, to find the approach which gives the best results for your learners, or the blend of approaches which seems most suitable. David Kolb's learning cycle can be helpful in understanding the learning process, and Peter Honey and Alan Mumford's 'Learning Styles Questionnaire' is a useful tool for identifying an individual's learning style.

4 Identify opportunities for coaching

In coaching it is important for the learner to try out skills in a work setting, so it will be necessary to identify a suitable occasion for the coaching session. Taking into consideration the priorities that have been identified, set a suitable time for the first session.

5 Carry out the coaching session

Bearing in mind the preferred learning styles identified earlier:

- give a clear and easy-to-follow demonstration, while explaining to the learner the details of what is happening and why

- watch for signs that the learner may have missed something – for example, by observing body language or asking questions

- build in summaries and reviews at appropriate points to ensure the learner grasps the key points

- let the learner try out the activity or behaviour for themselves, with accompanying support and reminders if needed

- provide the encouragement that all learners need and deserve when they are doing well.

6 Review progress and provide feedback

Help the learner reflect on what has gone well and where there is room for further development. Feedback is invaluable and can be a powerful motivating factor. It should be honest but sensitive, critical but constructive, and it must always focus on improvements and point the way forward.

7 Plan interim developments

Plan development activities for the learner to undertake between coaching sessions. Coaching should not be a spoon-feeding process; it is essential for the learner to be sufficiently motivated to develop the skills they have learned. Encourage the learner to identify opportunities to practise new skills. Improvement targets for practice sessions should be agreed before the close of the coaching session.

8 Monitor performance and progress

At the close of each session, discuss and review:

- the learner's success against the criteria and standards for acceptable performance agreed at the start
- how well the learner handles the learning process.

Plan the next steps. These may involve moving on to a further area for development or more coaching on the current task, if either the task or the learning objectives have not been met in full.

Devise a checklist as a means of objectively assessing long-term performance and improvement. Consider including such aspects as key milestones/dates to be reached; recording each coaching session and monthly/quarterly review dates; gaining feedback from both the learner and the coach; and making recommendations for the next steps in the development cycle. Such a record acts as a means of tracking performance for future reference and makes the whole process clearer and more transparent.

As a manager you should avoid:

- making assumptions about the learner's prior level of knowledge and skill
- confusing coaching with assessment
- telling the learner what to do, or taking over if they experience difficulties
- forgetting external criteria such as health and safety regulations or industry requirements.

Giving feedback as a coach

Feedback is a term adopted from the engineering sciences in which the output of a system is used to regulate or control the input to the system. In a coaching context, feedback gives others information about their activities, skills, abilities and behaviour with the aim of raising their awareness of how their behaviour affects others, and helping them to understand first, whether their behaviour has had the effect they intended, and second, how it should be changed to achieve the desired effect.

From time to time managers may have to give feedback to members of their teams, and this can include both praise and criticism. Sometimes they may view such an encounter with trepidation. However, it is important to remember that the role of a coach is to reflect their perceptions without judging, and there is no need to be apprehensive about this. The right approach can ensure that the risks of the feedback session going wrong are minimised and the desired outcomes are achieved.

Like all interviews, good communications skills are important in giving feedback successfully. Communication can be defined as the process of transferring ideas or thoughts from one person to another, for the purpose of creating understanding in the person receiving the communication. Two key skills of feedback, therefore, are questioning and listening. Coaching is a motivational activity, often seeking to encourage the person to gain new skills and knowledge. Any criticism needs to take this into account and generally be positive. This checklist focuses on the overall skill of giving feedback.

Action checklist

1 Prepare for the feedback session

Preparation for any feedback encounter is crucial. You need to think about the outcomes you want, what you are going to say and how you are going to say it. You need to consider where you are going to give the feedback and ensure you have allowed yourself sufficient time. You shouldn't rush it.

Your objectives should be:

- ownership of the feedback by the recipient
- a commitment to change where desired
- co-creation and agreement of an action plan for implementation after the feedback session.

The feedback conversation should be a participative exercise where everything that is said will be viewed as helpful and developmental. This means that the feedback should be carried out in a relaxed atmosphere, unhurried and free from tension, and characterised by openness and honesty. Judgemental, accusing and patronising statements will immediately provoke resistance. This is likely to lead to defensive behaviours, with the objectives of the interview not being achieved. Side by side, alongside a table, or across the corner of a table are good settings. A private and confidential location is essential.

2 Focus on communication skills

Any communication must involve a minimum of two people: the sender and the receiver. As the person giving the feedback, you should remember that although you should aim to be talking for only about 20% of the time, you are communicating as both the sender and the receiver, so you need to consider the communication process from both perspectives.

As the initial sender (or giver) of feedback, try to avoid misunderstandings by:

- working at sending clear, unambiguous messages – think about your use of words and the logic of the message; whether it is pitched at the appropriate level; your questioning technique; and your body language

- checking that the message has been understood as it was intended to be – ask the recipient of feedback to summarise what you have said; listen to what they are saying; and watch how they respond.

As the receiver, try to avoid misunderstandings by:

- actively listening to what has been said
- observing any non-verbal behaviour
- asking for clarification of any unclear verbal or non-verbal messages
- summarising your understanding at regular intervals.

A coach should adopt the following guidelines:

- Focus on the behaviour and not the person. This is the most important point. It helps to avoid any sense of personal attack, whether the feedback is reinforcing good behaviours or attempting to change undesired behaviours.
- Be assertive and aware of your rights as well as those of the other person.
- Don't be aggressive or overbearing; but don't be non-assertive or apologetic either.
- Be direct (not blunt) and to the point.
- Avoid sarcasm and demeaning comments.
- Avoid blaming the individual with aggressive 'you' statements.
- Display appropriate body language, especially in terms of eye contact, body positioning and physical mannerisms.
- Be specific about the good or bad behaviours and be non-judgemental.
- Mutually explore and possibly offer suggestions or options for improvement or change.

3 Develop your questioning skills

Coaches who develop the skill of questioning rather than telling should be able to use open questions to get the learner talking. Open questions begin with 'what,' 'why,' 'when,' 'how,' 'where' or 'who' and are difficult to answer with a 'yes' or a 'no'. Helping learners identify the situation for themselves is a powerful and effective way to give feedback and will greatly increase the chances of its being accepted.

4 Beginning the feedback conversation

At the start of the interview it is important to devote time to establishing rapport. The allotted timescale may vary, but the conversation should not be rushed. Any encounter that increases self-awareness can be threatening, and many recipients are conditioned to view it as a negative and not a positive process. 'It will tell me what I am poor at, not what I am good at' or 'It will prove I am not up to scratch' is the kind of thinking that may be displayed. The coach will need to combat this.

It is important to begin by explaining the situation. You could start by asking an open question such as:

- How do you think you did?
- How did you feel about that?
- What did you hope to achieve?
- How would you assess your performance?

It may be helpful for you to mentally rehearse your approach, particularly the opening, even to the extent of writing it out and repeating it to yourself several times so that you are familiar with it and say it naturally. You should aim to highlight any problems as early as possible in the conversation.

During the conversation it is advisable to:

- get to the point quickly and be specific. You should state what the problem is and, where appropriate, how the problem is affecting them, you, your customers, your work area or the team.

You should have specific facts at your disposal to support your comments

- own what you say. Use the 'I' word and take responsibility for what you are saying. Don't use 'you' – it is blaming.

These sorts of phrases are usually appropriate:

- I want
- I think
- I would like
- I don't like
- I know that

Some useful phrases are:

- The ratings indicate that
- The indications are that
- Measured against previous scores

Unhelpful phrases are:

- You are
- This is a poor rating on
- One area of weakness is
- I have rarely seen a performance that bad
- That was awful

Remember to focus on the behaviour and not the person. You should:

- use assertive body language. A loud voice, finger-wagging, an inability to look the recipient in the eye are not recommended; people are much more comfortable if you look at them directly in a calm, unemotional manner. However, make sure that you don't convey cold detachment in your endeavour to appear unemotional
- explore weaknesses or development areas by letting the person

identify the weakness or mistakes for themselves and considering the benefits of change

● explore suggestions for improvement. You should know what you want in terms of outcome, but you can ask for suggestions from the person before suggesting your own. They may well suggest what you want, which will increase ownership.

Useful phrases here are:

● What do you think you should do?

● How could you resolve this?

● What are the options?

Obtain (if appropriate) a commitment to change with the recognition that if change is possible, the onus is on the learner. Establish the level of support required from you as coach. If there are challenging issues, the individual may want to 'sleep on it', so be prepared to reconvene the following day.

5 Giving negative feedback

Many managers view giving criticism with distaste, being apprehensive about the response as well as their own feelings. You should remember, however, that many positive benefits can accrue from properly administered constructive criticism, and that problems must be confronted if future success is to be achieved. Remember also that there is probably greater potential to learn from our mistakes than from our successes. A feedback interview involving criticism should be constructive and not destructive, so that everything that is said is viewed as helpful and developmental.

6 Giving positive feedback

Work with the positives whenever you can. Praise conveys recognition of good behaviour and/or performance. As a coach, one of your roles is to help to motivate learners and reinforce good habits, behaviour and performance. Praise, if administered correctly, is a powerful way of doing this, because it recognises effort, helps make people feel valued and secure, and increases self-esteem and confidence.

While giving praise is more palatable than giving criticism, it can still cause embarrassment to both the giver and the recipient, and therefore may not be given as frequently as it should be. A coach needs to prepare well to get the learner to accept the praise as sincere, and to use it to reinforce good work so that it continues, with motivation levels increasing as a result.

At the interview it is advisable to:

- deliver your opening statement, which you should have rehearsed

- deliver the praise as soon as possible

- be specific by saying exactly what pleased you and how it affected you, your customers, your work area or the team – for example, 'All the estimates you have done for me this past month have been accurate, well presented, and accepted by the management team, which has reflected well on the department and myself'

- keep it short and to the point – don't gush and go over the top, as this may be perceived as insincere, and it may also devalue future praise; equally, don't adopt a patronising manner, as this will irritate the recipient

- use the 'I' word and take responsibility for what you are saying – so 'the company would like to place on record its appreciation of' is not as good as 'I appreciate'

- avoid belittling yourself by inflating others into gods and giants – for example, 'You've got more tact in your little finger than I've got in my whole body'

- use assertive body language – if you are calm and unemotional, look the recipient in the eye, smile and have an open posture, you won't go far wrong.

Remember: **it is not what you say but how you say it**.

As a manager you should avoid:

- destructive criticism
- being poorly prepared and rushing the feedback encounter
- ambiguous messages that lack clarity.

Devising a coaching programme

Typically, a coaching programme is a structured series of events aimed at overall performance improvement and increased personal and job satisfaction for an individual or team.

This checklist describes how to structure a coaching programme and introduces some of the major stages involved if the participants are to experience meaningful learning. The focus is on the coaching typically carried out by line managers to improve or manage performance in a specific task or job. This could relate to an individual employee or a team. A coaching programme is set up between the coach and the learners to realise this aim.

The experience and seniority of coaches vary. So to customise each programme for its recipients, coaches also need to consider the ways in which individuals learn and which learning methods to employ.

The stages to consider when devising a coaching programme for an individual or team are:

- diagnosis and exploration
- understanding
- considering learning methods
- developing a 'coaching contract'
- follow-up and review.

Action checklist

1 Diagnosis and exploration

For both individuals and teams, the first step is to make an initial diagnosis of strengths and weaknesses. You may need to consider other opinions, notably those of the learners. Let them decide on their own perception of the situation and give them ample opportunity to express their needs. Questioning, listening and observation skills are the principal requirements of a good coach.

Another important task is the setting of goals, which must be SMART (specific, measurable, actionable, realistic, timely or time-bound). You should agree both short-term and long-term goals, and the former should be a series of milestones along the route to the achievement of the latter. If the goals are proposed by the learners, so much the better – try to avoid imposing goals wherever possible. To monitor the learners' progress, it is necessary to record these goals, making all parties concerned fully aware of any timescales for achieving them.

2 Understanding

At this stage, the job of the coach is to help the learners to understand the magnitude of the problem and the challenges they face. They need to discover for themselves the limitations, demands and implications of what they are about to embark upon. Once they fully understand the situation, you should seek their agreement and commitment to the goals.

This stage will also involve consideration of how best to achieve the goals. By utilising your coaching skills, you should help the learners to identify the options, prioritise them and decide on the best way forward. However, sometimes you may feel that they have made the wrong choice. You should then use your skills to lead them to a better conclusion, rather than just stating your opinions and experiences in order to persuade them.

By the end of this stage, the learners should understand exactly what they are aiming for, the full implications of this, and how they hope to get there.

3 Considering learning methods

When planning the content of coaching sessions and the ways in which learning will be imparted, it is important to consider how individuals learn and to use various learning methods.

Learning occurs whenever new behaviour patterns are adopted or existing ones modified in a way that has some influence on future performance or attitudes. It is about a change in behaviour that is reasonably permanent and grows out of past experience.

Research conducted by the psychologist Albert Mehrabian indicates that learners retain approximately:

- 10% of what they read
- 20% of what they hear
- 30% of what they see
- 50% of what they both hear and use
- 70% of what they say
- 90% of what they see and do.

Though these percentages are only approximations, they do indicate that participants:

- learn faster by seeing and hearing than by hearing alone
- learn even faster when doing is added to seeing and hearing
- retain more of the things they do than of the things they are told.

This research indicates that effective learning must utilise experience – both through actually experiencing something and through analysing and sharing their experience for the benefit of all.

Of all the learning theories that have been developed, the theory of 'Experiential Learning' is perhaps the most useful for coaches. This is because it links experience with analysis to bring about behavioural change.

Experiential learning:

- puts the emphasis on the actual experiences that people go through as the starting point of the learning process
- focuses on the mental processes that individuals use to analyse the experience, including performance, emotions and feelings.

Experiential learning theory was developed in the 1970s by David Kolb, who suggested that learning follows a cycle with four distinct stages. The learning cycle was modified in the 1980s by Peter Honey and Alan Mumford, who linked the four stages in the cycle to four learning styles (see chart). Awareness of personal preferences in learning style is an important prerequisite for learning how to learn.

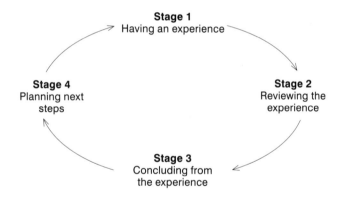

Figure 4: The experiental learning cycle

The cycle begins with an experience which could challenge existing views. This is then subject to reflection and observation to absorb the meaning of the experience. Only after time for reflection – to allow the brain to reprogram itself – should we conceptualise or seek to find the general principles that are derived from the initial experience. Lastly, the effective learner enters a stage of experimenting to test new knowledge and see whether it works in practice. Then the cycle begins again with the implementation of the new ideas and knowledge.

Some suggestions for applying this theory are:

- getting the learners to complete the Learning Styles Questionnaire (LSQ). This will help them and you to identify their preferred learning style, as well as their strengths and development areas

- designing experiences that are meaningful and using different methods. This will take learners around the cycle many times, thus reinforcing earlier learning.

4 Developing a 'coaching contract'

With appropriate methods of learning in mind, develop a form of 'coaching contract' for your coaching sessions. Specific steps in a specific timeframe are needed, with the learners having a positive, hands-on series of learning opportunities.

Do not try to be overly ambitious in a session. Learners need sufficient time to practise a new skill or improvement, and the coach needs to observe progress being made. Consequently, you should set small, achievable tasks; you should not require learners to make quantum leaps, which will involve a high level of failure and result in demotivation and lack of self-confidence.

The early sessions in a coaching programme are crucial to success. In these sessions, goals are defined and relationships between coaches and learners are developed. Progress will then be much smoother. Keep the focus on one goal at a time, and regularly evaluate progress to ensure that you are on course for the final goal. It is the responsibility of coaches to take actions related to the goals set and to monitor progress. At each milestone, take time out to praise and recognise achievement.

Any effective coaching programme will be subject to constraints. You will be structuring your programme within time limits and subject to the available resources. Therefore it is vital to set objectives that will make your sessions as effective as possible within the set boundaries.

It is important to finish on a positive note so that learners leave the session with a 'can do' rather than a 'can't do' attitude. Comments about previous achievements or recognition of the achievement of a milestone or of general contribution to the team will help you to build self-belief in the learners.

5 Follow-up and review

As in most processes, the final stage leads back into the first stage, but hopefully by this time you will have learnt from the experience and be much wiser. This final stage involves the following:

- finding out what people have learnt and how much they have achieved

- evaluating the performance of both the learners and the coach. As the coach, you need to give and receive feedback. Comments from peers, the learners and of course you as the coach can be involved. By skilful questioning you can help the learners to identify for themselves the reasons for success or failure. For example:
  - What did you/we do well?
  - What did you/we do badly?
  - What needs to change?
  - What have you/we learnt?

- practising 'positive discontent' – that is, letting the learners be proud of their achievements but not allowing them to 'rest on their laurels'. Look for ways to continually stretch them without being negative. If you have handled the process skilfully, the learners, flushed with success, will be keen to move forward with the next task.

If time permits, the learners can practise their new skills again. If this is not possible, it could form the starting point for the next session. As coach, you need to stay close to the situation and observe the learners in action soon. 'Come back next month and let me know how you got on' is not very helpful. Offers of help and support demonstrate interest and reinforce commitment on both sides.

As a manager you should avoid:

- adopting a directive approach
- trying to cover too much in one session
- assuming that everyone learns in the same way, at the same rate
- neglecting to recognise achievement
- failing to give ongoing support and encouragement.

Douglas McGregor
Theory X and theory Y

Introduction

Douglas McGregor (1906–64) followed a mostly academic career lecturing at Harvard University, Massachusetts Institute of Technology (MIT) and Antioch College, becoming the first Sloan Fellows Professor at MIT. Although, because of his early death, he was author of only a few publications, they have had a great impact. In 1993 McGregor was listed as the most popular management writer alongside Henri Fayol (Andreas Huczynski, *Management Gurus – What Makes Them and How to Become One*). American management gurus such as Rosabeth Moss Kanter, Warren Bennis and Tom Peters, whose work has had much influence on current learning and practice, agree that much of modern management thinking goes back to McGregor, especially the implications of his thoughts on leadership.

McGregor believed that managers' basic beliefs have a dominant influence on the way that organisations are run. Managers' assumptions about the behaviour of people are central to this. He argues that these assumptions fall into two broad categories: theory X and theory Y. These findings were detailed in *The Human Side of Enterprise*, first published in 1960.

Theory X and theory Y describe two views of people at work and may be used to describe two opposing management styles.

Theory X: the traditional view of direction and control

Theory X is based on the following assumptions:

- The average human being has an inherent dislike of work and will avoid it if possible.

- Because of this, most people must be coerced, controlled, directed, and threatened with punishment to get them to put adequate effort towards the achievement of organisational objectives.

- The average human being prefers to be directed, wishes to avoid responsibility, has relatively little ambition, and wants security above all.

A theory X management style therefore requires close, firm supervision with clearly specified tasks and the threat of punishment or the promise of greater pay as motivating factors. A manager working under these assumptions will employ autocratic controls, which can lead to mistrust and resentment from those they manage. McGregor acknowledges that this constitutes a damning statement about the 'mediocrity of the masses'. He acknowledges too that the 'carrot and stick' approach can have a place, but it will not work when the needs of people are predominantly social and egoistic.

Theory Y: the integration of individual and organisational goals

Theory Y is based on the following assumptions:

- The expenditure of physical and mental effort in work is as natural as play or rest. The average human being does not inherently dislike work. Depending upon controllable conditions, work may be a source of satisfaction or a source of punishment.

- External control and the threat of punishment are not the only means of bringing about effort towards organisational objectives.

Human beings will exercise self-direction and self-control in the service of objectives to which they are committed.

- Commitment to objectives is a function of the rewards associated with their achievement. The most significant of such rewards, such as the satisfaction of ego and self-actualisation needs, can be direct products of effort directed towards organisational objectives.

- The average human being learns, under proper conditions, not only to accept but also to seek responsibility. Avoidance of responsibility, lack of ambition and emphasis on security are generally consequences of experience, not inherent human characteristics.

- The capacity to exercise a relatively high degree of imagination, ingenuity and creativity in the solution of organisational problems is widely, not narrowly, distributed in the population.

- Under the conditions of modern industrial life, the intellectual potential of the average human being is only partially utilised. Theory Y assumptions can lead to more cooperative relationships between managers and workers. A theory Y management style seeks to establish a working environment in which the personal needs and objectives of individuals can relate to, and harmonise with, the objectives of the organisation.

In *The Human Side of Enterprise* McGregor recognised that theory Y was not a panacea for all ills. By highlighting theory Y, he hoped instead to achieve the abandonment by management of the limiting assumptions of theory X and a consideration of the techniques involved in theory Y.

Theory into practice

Abraham Maslow viewed McGregor as a mentor and was a strong supporter of theories X and Y. He put theory Y (that people want to work, achieve and take responsibility) into practice in a Californian electronics factory. However, he found that an organisation driven solely by theory Y could not succeed, as some sense of direction and structure was required. Instead, Maslow advocated an improved version of theory Y, which involved an element of structured security and direction taken from theory X.

Maslow's negative experience with implementing theory Y must be balanced against that of McGregor himself at a Procter & Gamble plant in Georgia, where he introduced theory Y through the concept of self-directed teams. This plant was found to be a third more profitable than any other Procter & Gamble plant; it was kept a trade secret until the mid-1990s.

Before he died, McGregor began to develop a further theory which addressed the criticisms made of theories X and Y: that they were mutually incompatible. Ideas he proposed as part of this theory included lifetime employment, concern for employees (both inside and outside the working environment), decision by consensus and commitment to quality. He tentatively called it theory Z. Before it could be widely published, McGregor died and the ideas faded.

Theory Z

The work on theory Z that McGregor began was not completely forgotten. During the 1970s, William Ouchi began to expound its principles by comparing and contrasting Japanese (type J) and American (type A) organisations.

Type A organisations tended to offer short-term employment, specialised careers (with rapid promotion) and individual decision-making and responsibility. Type J firms, by contrast, mirrored the ethos of Japanese society: collectivism and stability rather than individuality. Those American firms that shared type J characteristics (and indeed had more in common with type J organisations) were described as type Z (examples included Hewlett-Packard and Procter & Gamble).

Leadership

Before McGregor, most writing about leadership focused on the qualities and characteristics of 'Great People', in the hope that, if those qualities were identified, they could be emulated.

McGregor argued that there were other variables involved in leadership, including the attitudes and needs of the followers, the nature and structure of the organisation itself, and the social, economic and political environment. For McGregor, leadership was not a property of the individual, but a complex relationship among these variables. He was one of the first to argue that leadership was more about the relationship between the leader and the situation they faced, than merely the characteristics of the leader alone.

In perspective

The Human Side of Enterprise marked a watershed in management thinking, which had previously been dominated by the scientific approach of Frederick Taylor, and laid the foundations for the current people-centred view of management.

Theory Y has been criticised for being too idealistic, but an examination of the six tenets of theory Y shows that much modern thinking can be traced back to McGregor:

- 1 Work – as a source of satisfaction – means accepting that people need to know not just what or how, but why. The adoption of meaningful objectives is one of the keys to self-motivation.
- 2–4 Ownership, commitment and responsibility are three of the flagships of empowerment.
- 5–6 Encouragement for people to be fully exercised in the solution of organisational problems is central to action learning, total quality management, strategic thinking and knowledge exploitation.

As noted earlier, Moss Kanter (empowerment), Bennis

(leadership) and Peters (excellence and chaos) all acknowledge their debt to McGregor.

Criticisms

Contemporary and subsequent commentaries on McGregor's theories have tended to see them as black and white. Harold Geneen, former president and CEO of ITT, commented that although theories X and Y propose a neat summary of business management, no company is run in strict accordance with either one or the other. Peter Drucker said that theory X sees people as immature, whereas theory Y sees them striving towards adulthood.

The two contrasting theories are perhaps best seen as two polarising forces with which managers have to grapple. Robert Blake and Jane Mouton expressed this in terms of the managerial grid, where managers constantly have to balance the drives and forces between task – getting things done – and people – how best to get them done for the benefit of the organisation and the individuals doing them.

Although theory Y has been held up as an unachievable aim – with the individual and the organisation having convergent aspirations – the successful cases where this has been attempted are growing. It is what organisations are trying to do through continuous improvement, continuous professional development and participation schemes operating in climates of empowerment.

It is not going too far to say that *The Human Side of Enterprise* recognises that we cannot actually motivate people, but we do have to acknowledge the opposing forces at play. What we can do is attempt to create the right climate, environment or working conditions for motivation to be enabled.

Mentoring in practice

Mentoring is understood here as a form of employee development whereby a trusted and respected person – the mentor – uses their experience to offer guidance, encouragement and support to another person – the mentee.

Mentoring is a relationship in which one person (the mentor), who is usually more experienced and often more senior, supports another (the learner or mentee) with regular guidance, feedback and confidential discussion, so that they can become more self-aware, knowledgeable and able to develop their potential and capability. A mentoring relationship may be informal, or it can be a more formal arrangement between two people who respect and trust each other. It does not usually involve bringing together a trainer and a trainee or a line management arrangement, where seniority comes into play. The mentor can be any person with appropriate experience, ability and knowledge. Their role is to listen, ask questions, probe for facts, act as a source of information and guidance, and signpost opportunities for learning from which the mentee can benefit. The aim of mentoring is to help mentees form their own views, develop different perspectives, grow personally and work towards or achieve their next intended goals.

Mentoring is a popular development tool. It is widely used in education and in health services. In the UK, a national mentoring scheme has helped unemployed people aged 18–24 to work with mentors from their chosen career or industry path. Apprenticeships are also based on a form of mentoring, with an onsite supervisor available to support apprentices through their learning journeys. As a development process, mentoring has advantages for mentors, mentees and organisations.

For mentors it offers:

- the opportunity to help and guide others in their career development
- increased job satisfaction, sense of value and status
- honing and development of the mentor's skills in management and leadership.

For mentees it offers:

- a visible demonstration of how the mentee is valued by the mentor
- an objective and safe source of support in the development of new skills and directions
- access to someone who understands their industry or organisation's culture and ways of working.

For organisations it offers:

- a cost-effective way to support succession planning and develop human potential
- better staff retention and recruitment prospects
- improved communication and acclimatisation of employees to the organisation's culture.

Action checklist

1 Check the mentor has the appropriate skills

It is essential for the mentor to have:

- good listening skills
- questioning skills – open, closed, probing, etc.
- the ability to suspend judgement and prejudice, and avoid driving the mentee in a single direction

- the ability to give both positive and negative feedback in a constructive and motivational way
- skill in helping to define objectives and plan ways of achieving them
- the ability to signpost opportunities for the mentee, drawing on other people's skills and experiences.

The mentor must also be someone with experience who can offer viewpoints from a valued perspective and open doors for the mentee. If necessary, mentors will need training and development to sharpen and refine their skills.

2 Clarify the relationship

Ensure that both mentee and mentor are clear on what the relationship is – and is not – about. This will avoid later confusion and disappointment. Consider safety and protection issues for both parties, and whether the mentor needs to apply for a CRB (Criminal Records Bureau) check (especially if the mentee is under 18, has special needs, or is vulnerable in any way). In the UK, the Mentoring and Befriending Foundation provides publications and good practice examples for mentoring.

If appropriate, consider drafting a mentoring contract, with specifications that include:

- the respective roles, responsibilities and commitment
- planning for the likely number and frequency of contacts, and for review and amending as required
- the required sharing of personal data, such as telephone numbers and email addresses
- an emphasis on the importance of confidentiality within the relationship.

Remember that the mentor's aim should be to support mentees in developing themselves – not to get them to adopt the mentor's ideas. Dependency is to be avoided at all stages.

3 Open the relationship

Recognise that, in the early stages, the mentor will take more of a lead. Later, as the mentee's confidence and understanding grows, the balance will shift. Set objectives for what the mentoring process is to achieve, and make these achievable, specific, relevant and time-limited. Also distinguish between short- and long-term goals that will need thought and consideration, and discuss ways of tackling these.

4 Develop the relationship

At the start of each mentoring session, and whenever the mentee achieves a milestone, review their success and identify what they learned about themselves and the process. Ask the mentee:

- What happened?
- Why?
- What was learned from the experience?
- What will you do differently the next time you are faced with a similar issue?

Identify jointly what needs to be explored in order to achieve the mentee's objective(s). Compare the desired outcome with the current situation, identify gaps and outline what needs to happen to bridge them.

If an objective is knowledge-based, or attitudinal, the action needed may be harder to pin down. So explore options, discuss experiences, and always leave mentees in a position to decide on what they can do for themselves.

If an objective is skill-based, break the required action down into milestones – small, self-contained 'chunks' – so that each one can be tackled as a manageable entity. This will build in opportunities for regular progress reviews and for success to be recognised and celebrated.

Select and agree appropriate actions that will assist in achieving the objectives, such as learning experiences that can be provided or facilitated by the mentor, knowledge that can be passed from mentor to mentee, or an increase in the self-awareness of the mentee through discussion and feedback.

At the end of each mentoring session, clarify what has been achieved, and be precise about what is to happen between this session and the next – especially if the mentor is to make arrangements on the mentee's behalf. Ensure that control of the mentee's development passes increasingly from the mentor to the mentee. This is essential, as it will ensure that the mentee is capable of acting independently when the mentoring process comes to an end.

5 End the relationship

Mentoring relationships between people outside work may exist for years. However, it is important to recognise that, in work, there is likely to be a point when mentoring ends and the objectives are achieved. When this point is reached, celebrate the success with a final review of the progress made.

As a manager you should avoid:

- assuming that any line manager can fulfil the role of a mentor
- assuming that an individual's direct line manager is an appropriate mentor
- disclosing information that is obtained while mentoring others
- being afraid, as a mentor, to be open about yourself. If a mentor doesn't know the answer to a question asked by the mentee, they should admit it and come to an agreement with the mentee on how they will address the issue
- trying to be over-directive – the mentoring journey is one of guided self-exploration.

  To be successful with mentoring, try to:
- ensure that the mentee finds the mentor suitable, and can respect, trust and open up to him or her

- concentrate on the mentee's needs and aims, and allow flexibility in the approach
- remember that a key part of the mentor's role is to open doors to other people's experience and learning
- ensure that each session starts with a review and ends with a clear action plan
- control the relationship and adjust as necessary so that the mentee has increasing responsibility.

Counselling your colleagues

Counselling involves one person using a set of skills to help another clarify concerns, come to terms with feelings, take responsibility for difficulties and begin to resolve problems or issues. Counselling does not mean giving advice, or providing or managing solutions to the problems experienced by the colleague. Counselling techniques are related to the mentoring process, where mentors may sometimes need to take a counselling approach.

Within the context of their work roles, managers may sometimes be required to help and support their colleagues at times of crisis or difficulty. At such times, using counselling skills can be helpful. It can take several years of training and supervised practical experience to become a professional counsellor. Although few managers have this level of qualification, many of the skills employed by counsellors can be put to use in the workplace.

Action checklist

1 Check your organisation's personnel policies

Some organisations have formal arrangements for counselling, so it is important to ensure that you are not contravening any policies by offering counselling. For example, your organisation may offer counselling through an employee assistance programme (EAP), as part of a package of employee benefits.

2 Decide on a suitable location

It is essential to choose somewhere private, quiet, free from interruption and appropriate to the nature of the discussion. To help put your colleague at ease, try to avoid a formal office setting with a desk between you. Position a clock somewhere appropriate (not behind your seat), so that you can keep an eye on the time without making this obvious. Ensure you will not be disturbed by putting an 'engaged' sign on the door, and divert your telephone to avoid interruptions.

3 Ensure there is sufficient time for the meeting

If you know you must end your meeting at a particular time, inform your colleague of this at the outset. To make sure you have sufficient time for the session, it is often sensible to book a meeting (perhaps a day in advance). Even if there is no particular reason for a fixed time limit, it is often useful to set one of about an hour. This will help to prevent the discussion continuing for an extended period in a non-constructive way, going over the same ground again and again without making any progress towards a positive outcome.

4 Consider your feelings towards your colleague

Before the meeting, it is essential to examine your personal feelings towards your colleague and put them to one side. Whether or not you like the colleague or have a personal affinity with them is irrelevant to the counselling session.

5 Open the meeting by explaining the framework

At the beginning of the counselling session it is essential to lay down some ground rules. These may include:

- **expectations for the discussion** – you will not be able to provide advice or guidance or solve any problems for your colleague, so clarify what can realistically be expected

- **time limitations** – state again what these are, and whether you will offer one or more follow-up sessions if needed

- **note taking** – stress that any notes taken are for your own use and will not be disclosed to a third party

- **confidentiality** – assure your colleague that everything discussed will remain confidential, unless there is a risk that they may cause harm to themselves or others. This should encourage your colleague to speak freely and openly and prevent them from being overly reticent through fear of repercussions later. Explain that the only exception to this will be if you both agree that something needs to be discussed with another party.

6 Begin to explore the issues with your colleague

The format of each session will depend on the needs of the individual – there is no set formula that will fit every occasion. However, the following skills are essential to ensure that issues are explored fully.

Listen actively

What does your colleague feel? What is their point of view? What is happening to them, in their view? What do they do (or not do)? It is essential to understand that your colleague's view of the facts or situation will be more important to them than the facts themselves, and that their behaviour may not reflect their true feelings. By rephrasing and reflecting back the concerns expressed by your colleague, you demonstrate that you have listened to what is being said. At the same time, active listening enables you to seek clarification of the issues involved. Summarising what has been said at regular intervals helps both parties remain focused.

Empathise

Empathy is not the same as sympathy. Empathy means you understand and acknowledge the individual's feelings about the situation confronting them without having to take their side or agree with everything they are saying. Empathy can help encourage your colleague to be more honest and precise when describing the issues.

Ask questions

There are many reasons to ask questions, and many different types of questions that may be asked. In counselling sessions, questions can clarify your understanding of the issues and help you focus on areas you think may be important. Asking questions also shows that you are taking a genuine interest in the other person. Open, closed and delving questions are particularly valuable in counselling sessions. Open questions can help your colleague begin to discuss an issue, and can give you information on how they feel. Closed questions help you establish facts, but they often lead to short answers. Delving questions enable you to probe an issue more fully and can help draw out the broader picture.

Challenge

By gently challenging statements made by your colleague when necessary, you can help them explore the situation they face and their response to it more closely. It is useful to challenge if the discussion seems to be going round in circles, your colleague appears to have an unrealistic self-image (either too positive or, more commonly, too negative) or they contradict themselves. You should use this technique with care, however, and ensure that trust is well established within the counselling relationship before challenging or confronting any issues or discrepancies.

Challenging statements may be phrased in this way: 'You say that you are struggling with your current project, yet I see you as meeting all its objectives and timescales. Why do you think there is a difference in our views?' A good rule of thumb is to always be gentle and supportive in using your 'challenge' skills.

7 Recognise situations that are beyond your help

In certain circumstances it may be necessary to refer your colleague to professional counsellors or organisations that may be better qualified to help them. Find sources of information and contact details of appropriate people, for example telephone book or local reference library. Your HR department may have some information, but be sure not to break confidence with your colleague if you speak to HR.

8 Help your colleague solve problems by setting objectives for action

Counselling does not mean that the counsellor provides solutions to the issues raised by the colleague. It does, however, involve the counsellor in the process of problem-solving. Problems and possible causes will have been identified during the discussion. It is now necessary to help your colleague set specific objectives to help tackle them. It is important to set timescales for any actions decided on and agree on a means of monitoring progress.

9 Close the session in an appropriate manner

Warn your colleague approximately ten minutes before the session is due to end. Ask if there is anything else they want to mention before you close the session. Then summarise what has been discussed and what actions have been agreed upon. When appropriate arrange a follow-up session.

As a manager you should avoid:

- letting personal feelings intrude on the discussion
- taking on the responsibility for solving problems
- being judgemental in what you say
- being afraid to refer a colleague to a professional if you feel it necessary.

Managing (your relationship with) your boss

Managing your boss is about developing a relationship of trust, respect and mutual support, which enables you to perform well within your job role and to develop your skills, knowledge and career. It means acknowledging who is the boss but retaining the ability to do the best you can for the organisation, the team and yourself. A good working relationship between a manager and his or her boss should involve fairness, mutual respect, trust and rapport as well as open and honest communication. The key word is 'manage', implying an ongoing process rather than a one-off activity.

The relationship you have with your boss plays a fundamental role in your ability to do your job well. In fact your relationship with your boss is the most important workplace relationship you have. Putting effort into building a productive and communicative working relationship with your boss ensures that you both know what is feasible and possible, and contributes to achieving the results that matter to you both. Good working relationships improve self-esteem, aid your personal development and put you in a strong position to overcome any problems or conflicts that may arise.

The relationship between manager and boss needs to be actively managed. It is not just a case of being pleasant or getting along well together – what is being managed is the relationship, not the individual.

It is important to take the time and trouble to talk to each other.

This will help you form an alliance and work together towards common goals. It will also give you a better understanding of your manager's objectives and values. This in turn will enable you to support your manager in his or her weaker areas. However, be wary of encouraging your boss to think that an idea you contributed was actually theirs.

This checklist will help those who wish, or need, to manage the relationship with their boss more effectively. Remember to appraise and review your current work, future goals and the interaction you have with your manager at regular intervals to ensure that a good working relationship is maintained.

Action checklist

1 Communicate clearly

Prevention is better than cure, and effective communication prevents a lot of misunderstandings and breakdowns in relationships. Make sure that you share information in a timely way, regularly and in adequate detail. Pay attention to formal communication, but also ensure you simply talk and compare notes from time to time. Don't be afraid of asking for help if you need it.

2 Identify any blockages

Think about what may be blocking the way to a good working relationship. Consider your boss's behaviour and personal characteristics. Both can have a significant bearing on the development and quality of your relationship. Also be mindful that your behaviour will influence how your boss behaves towards you too. Leader–member exchange (LMX) theory supports this notion, arguing that a person's perception of their boss may be at odds with how other members of the team perceive their leader. In a similar way, your boss may behave differently with your colleagues than with you. When evaluating the relationship, do so within the context of how well or badly others get on with your boss. This will help you identify whether it is your behaviour or attitude that may be adversely affecting the quality of your relationship.

There may be other 'blockages' to a good working relationship – you may have trouble communicating, or find it hard to express your opinions or discuss workload issues. Identify what triggers these problems, being honest about your own weaknesses. Also consider which aspects of the relationship work well. Build upon these and work on reducing problems in other areas.

3 Identify your boss's leadership style

The way in which your boss acts or behaves towards you can also be affected by their leadership style, be it transactional or transformational. Your boss may take a bureaucratic, charismatic, dictatorial, consultative, or laissez-faire approach to leadership, any of which can affect your relationship with them. A specific style or mix of styles will require different approaches from you. Consider also your boss's 'thinking' style. It's no surprise that we get on well with some people, especially those who think like us, but others can easily rub us up the wrong way. Try to figure out whether your boss focuses on minutiae or the 'big picture', is reactive or proactive, likes or hates change, is a right-brain or left-brain person.

4 Identify your boss's objectives and values

Think about what is important to your boss and work hard on these areas. The two main areas to pay attention to are:

- what, in the eyes of your manager, the key objectives are and what support you can give towards achieving them
- what personal values your boss holds dear, such as customer care. Work on supporting these values and don't do things that are contrary to them.

You should also consider your boss's motives and personal ambitions, such as promotions and achievements they want to gain for themselves. Think about where your boss has come from in terms of former employment, educational background and so on. How much is your boss interested in the organisation compared with his or her own career development? Be wary of evidently self-interested values, such as personal status. Having an understanding of such matters will help you to understand their motives and their approach to managing you.

5 Clarify boundaries of responsibility

Sort out with your boss exactly what decisions you can make:

- after discussion with your boss
- on your own but reporting to your boss afterwards
- on your own with no need to report.

Lack of clarity can be a major source of conflict and friction. If you are clear about your sphere of responsibility, you will gain confidence in decision-making and avoid the need to keep referring small matters to your boss. Constant pestering runs the risk of irritating the boss and giving the impression that you lack confidence in your job.

6 Tackle the simple issues

Look through the problems you have identified and decide which will be easy to resolve. Can small administrative problems be addressed by simply introducing a new system? Discuss minor sensitivities (such as opening the office window, working in silence or with background noise) with your boss and try to reach a compromise. Don't waste time reporting minor successes.

Work overload is a common cause of conflict. Don't take on work you can't manage – be honest, but remember your boss's objectives and always suggest an alternative solution. Don't underestimate yourself or your point of view. If you don't have faith in your ability to do a good job and develop in your role, your boss certainly won't.

7 Tackle longer-term issues with assertiveness

Some blockages cannot be dealt with overnight. Concentrate on building a stronger relationship with your boss over the long term. This means being assertive but not aggressive. Express your point of view, respect your boss's opinions and work to find mutually acceptable solutions to existing problems. This will improve your relationship and help you handle difficult situations more effectively in the future. Resolve not to go over your boss's head, however attractive this may seem. If you feel blocked, tackle the issues directly to avoid creating more problems later.

8 Focus on loyalty and support

Focus on supporting your boss in any weak areas they may have, without making it too obvious that you are doing so. Find out which parts of the business they enjoy and are good at, and which they don't like doing or perhaps don't have the skills to deal with. Make yourself indispensable. Show you are keen to learn skills that complement your boss's skills. Win their trust by achieving things they value. Together you can become a winning team.

9 Think about how others see you

People make big assumptions about your abilities from the way you look or the way you present yourself. They may assume that a scruffy, untidy-looking person is disorganised, bad at their job and generally unreliable. Look smart. Smile and demonstrate a positive approach. Celebrate your successes. Make sure that your manager knows when you have done well and understand that your success reflects on them too.

10 Take advantage of opportunities that present themselves

Keep your eye on the big picture and not just the task in hand. Don't use work overload as an excuse to avoid activities such as attending conferences or meeting senior directors. Weigh up the short-term disadvantages against the potential longer-term value to the organisation. Think about what these opportunities could contribute to your development and what you could learn from them.

11 Communicate your own agenda

There's no need to be abrasive, but a modicum of repetition may be useful in making sure that your ideas are heard. This may relate to specific projects or ongoing work, but think about the bigger picture too. What do you want to learn? Where do you want your career to go? Instead of always playing your boss's tune, develop joint objectives.

12 Review issues and actions, and plan future development

Review issues which are important to you and discuss them with your boss. They should matter to your boss because if you fail, so will your boss. Discuss problems before they get out of hand and have some ideas for solutions ready for discussion.

13 When relationships are genuinely difficult

Most of this checklist is valid if you have a boss who acts reasonably. Sometimes you may be faced with a difficult boss. Three of the worst types are the bully, the sexually harassing boss and the glory-stealing boss. It is not easy to deal with any of these, although employment law does provide some protection in respect of the first two. Techniques such as keeping records, collecting evidence and bypassing your boss can be useful to deal with the glory-stealer.

14 Nip conflict in the bud

If conflict breaks out between you and your boss, handle it. Don't run away or tackle anger with anger.

15 Review the relationship

Sit down from time to time and ask yourself: 'How are we doing?' Make an assessment of your interactions, so that you both know how things stand, and can work to improve and maintain the underlying relationship. Use instances of success or failure as a vehicle for reviewing the relationship. Work out what to repeat in the future and what to do differently next time.

As a manager you should avoid:

- being passive – never questioning what your boss wants and failing to put forward personal viewpoints
- being aggressive – fighting fire with fire rarely works
- going over your boss's head if it can possibly be avoided
- ignoring problems and avoiding any discussion of them
- blaming your boss for 'blockages' in the relationship without also looking at your own behaviour
- failing to communicate openly.

Handling conflict

Conflict arises from the clash of competing ideas and personal interests. There are many sources of conflict in the workplace: differences of opinion, dissatisfaction with working conditions or remuneration, excessive workloads, lack of recognition or promotion, perceptions of discriminatory or unfair treatment, feelings of insecurity, fear of redundancy, clashes of personality, misunderstandings or breakdowns in communication, differing expectations of what constitutes appropriate behaviour, to name but a few.

Conflict may be between managers and their staff, or between team members, departments, or managers. Conflict may be expressed openly, but it may also be hidden, in the form of irritation, resentment, loss of morale and lack of commitment. Hidden conflict is easy to miss but can nonetheless be damaging. If nothing is done to address the underlying issues, conflict, whether open or hidden, may escalate – from gossip, backbiting and criticism to shouting matches, threats and possible violence. Such consequences can often be prevented by taking early action to address the issues. This checklist focuses on steps for handling interpersonal conflict within the workplace, as opposed to conflict with customers, which requires a different form of resolution.

Disagreements, differences of opinion and conflicting perspectives on key issues inevitably arise in any context where people are working together, especially in a competitive business environment. While not all conflict is negative – creative solutions and new ideas can often emerge from the cut and thrust of debate – conflict can frequently become destructive. For example, negative emotions may be stirred up, poisoning the atmosphere, undermining morale, creating stress and destroying workplace relationships. This can result in a lack of motivation that will have an adverse effect on performance. If ignored, conflict can escalate or spread to affect others. If conflicts are not resolved, the situation may deteriorate, leading to litigation and damaging the organisation's reputation. Conflict can be costly in terms of time and money. It is therefore vital to manage conflict constructively.

Action checklist

1 Be aware of conflict

Keep your eyes and ears open for changes in workplace climate and any early signs of developing conflict. Don't turn a blind eye to symptoms of hidden conflict. Conflict can be safely ignored only if it is momentary and unlikely to escalate. Ignoring conflict may be an easy option initially, but in most cases it does not help and will create a situation that is more difficult to resolve later.

2 Prepare yourself to take action

Stay calm and ensure that you are able to take a considered, rational and impartial approach to the situation. If you are personally involved, you may need to ask someone else to handle the issue.

- Avoid the temptation of the instinctive reactions 'fight or flight'. Neither of these approaches is constructive: 'flight' avoids the issue and doesn't resolve the conflict; 'fight' provokes greater conflict and may intimidate the parties involved.

- Avoid passive behaviour – do not take an apologetic stance and accept all points of view whether they are right or wrong.

- Avoid aggressive behaviour – do not take an authoritarian approach and fail to listen to reasoned argument.

- Aim to take an assertive stance by treating all parties with respect and listening to all points of view.

- Take care with your use of language and your body language while dealing with people involved in conflict.

- Listen carefully to any evidence offered and take notes.

- Be neutral.

3 Investigate the situation

Take time to find out what has happened, who is involved, how people are feeling and what the issues are. Don't prejudge the issue or jump to conclusions. Speak individually and confidentially to those involved and listen attentively to make sure you understand their point of view. This can be checked by summarising what they have said and reflecting it back to them. Try to identify any underlying causes of conflict that may not be immediately obvious. For example, a member of staff may be in apparent conflict with colleagues, while the root cause is their perception that a supervisor is treating them unfairly. Be aware that those involved may have differing perceptions of the situation. Avoid being pulled into the middle of the argument and taking sides.

4 Decide on your approach

Having examined the situation, decide what action would be appropriate:

- Is this a serious matter or relatively trivial? Could it become serious?

- Should organisational discipline or grievance procedures be invoked?

- Is the matter within your sphere of authority or should it be referred to a superior?

- Are any legal issues involved?

- Would the participation of a trade union representative be appropriate?

- Would it be best to make a ruling on the issue yourself, or would an informal gathering to discuss the problem be helpful? Will the parties accept your ruling?

- Is time needed for heated emotions to subside before moving forward?

  In most cases a mutually agreed solution will be more effective than an imposed solution, which may leave all parties dissatisfied. Consider how you can get those involved together to exchange views and explore the issues. Do you have access to mediators (formal or informal)?

5 Let everyone have their say

If you are able to get the parties together, you may be able to reach a satisfactory solution. Take a positive, friendly and assertive approach to the meeting and set ground rules for the session. Assertive behaviour will encourage the parties to express their thoughts honestly and openly, understand the causes of conflict and find solutions. Make sure that all parties have a chance to explain their views and concerns. People will be more willing to relinquish entrenched positions and consider compromise if they feel that their view has been understood and their concerns taken on board.

6 Identify options and agree on a way forward

This is the most important and often the most difficult part of the process. The following steps may be helpful in reaching agreement:

- Create an atmosphere where all parties are able to speak openly and honestly and where they can make concessions without losing face.

- Acknowledge emotional issues, as these are at the heart of it and thus need to be resolved. However, don't allow them to take over.

- Consider carefully the extent to which you need to control the meeting and intervene in the discussion.

- Explore the reasons for the disagreement.

- Identify any misconceptions or misunderstandings that are blocking progress.

- Encourage the parties to examine their positions and identify any common ground with others. For example, could they have got the message wrong?

- Look for points that may be negotiable and seek win/win solutions that take the interests of all parties into account.

- Ask the parties to put forward preferred solutions.

- Allow time for reflection.

- Assess each option and help the parties to agree on which represents the best way forward.

- Secure the commitment of all parties to any agreement and agree a review point.

  If no progress is made, a period of reflection may help, but ultimately it may be necessary to bring in another manager or to consider external assistance from a specialist in mediation, ADR (alternative dispute resolution) or arbitration.

7 Implement what has been agreed

It is important to ensure that everyone is clear about what has been decided and takes personal responsibility for any actions that have been agreed. In some cases a written agreement may be appropriate. Take great care with any situations, such as public apologies, which could cause embarrassment to the parties involved.

8 Evaluate how things are going

Don't assume that the issue has been fully resolved. Continue to keep an eye on the situation and evaluate how well the solution is working. If the problem reappears, it may be necessary to take further action.

9 Consider preventative strategies for the future

Think about the lessons that can be learnt from the conflict and the way it was handled. What could be done better next time? How could you develop your conflict management skills? You may wish to consider training in influencing, mediation or dispute resolution techniques for yourself or a colleague.

Looking at the broader context, consider what action can be taken to improve working relationships and encourage a culture of open communication and consultation. Consider whether an organisational procedure for dispute resolution or mediation is needed. Think about whether there is something about the way the unit works that encourages this conflict behaviour and that can be 'fixed'.

As a manager you should avoid:

- ignoring signs of growing conflict among team members
- jumping to conclusions about the source of conflict before investigating thoroughly
- intervening too early or pre-empting discussion by imposing your own solution.

Warren Bennis
Leadership guru

Introduction

Warren Bennis's career has been extremely wide-ranging and has covered various areas. He worked as an educator, writer, administrator and consultant, and authored or co-authored many books on different topics. He has carried out highly respected work in the areas of small-group dynamics, change in social systems, T-groups and sensitivity training, and during the 1960s became a recognised futurologist. Bennis wrote his first article on leadership in 1959, and he has become a widely accepted authority on the subject since 1985, when *Leaders* was published.

Life and career

Bennis was born in New York in 1925 and educated at Antioch College and the Massachusetts Institute of Technology (MIT). During the Second World War he served in the army, and was the youngest infantry officer to be involved in European operations. Later, he studied group dynamics, and during the 1950s was involved in the US National Training Laboratories teamworking experiments. His early work was in organisational development.

Bennis, like Abraham Maslow and Charles Handy, both of whom he knew, was a great admirer of Douglas McGregor and his 'theory Y' approach to motivation. He became close to McGregor and was strongly influenced by him, and his career followed McGregor's to some extent. He was a student at Antioch College when McGregor was president; and in 1959 McGregor recruited him to set up a new department for organisation studies at MIT.

In the late 1960s, Bennis moved from academic research and teaching to administration for a time. He became provost at the State University of New York (SUNY), Buffalo, in 1967, staying there until 1971, when he moved to take on the post of president of the University of Cincinnati.

As an administrative leader from 1967 to 1978, he attempted to put McGregor's motivation theories into practice, and found the theory unworkable without some adaptation in the form of strengthened structure and direction. In an autobiographical book, *An Invented Life: Reflections on Leadership and Change* (1993), Bennis said that he felt a great sense of powerlessness as an administrative leader, despite the supposed power of his official status.

A student of the future

During the 1960s, Bennis became known as a student of the future, and predicted (with co-author Philip Slater in a March 1964 article, 'Democracy Is Inevitable', for *Harvard Business Review*) the downfall of communism in the face of inevitable democracy. By the mid-1960s, he was predicting the demise of bureaucratic organisation. His 1968 book, *The Temporary Society*, explored new forms of organisation, advocating an 'adhocracy' of free-moving project teams as a necessity for future organisations. This idea has since been taken up by other writers, such as Alvin Toffler and Henry Mintzberg.

In an adhocracy, responsibility and leadership are distributed to groups or taskforces on the basis of the relevance of members' qualifications or abilities for the specific task or purpose of the group. For Bennis, adhocracy was an important concept as a counter to hierarchy, centralised control and bureaucratic organisation.

In his early book on leadership, *The Unconscious Conspiracy*

(1976), he highlights how leaders can positively influence others to bring about change. His most distinctive ideas on the subject, however, partly grew out of the broad, general response to a landmark *Harvard Business Review* article of 1977 by Abraham Zaleznik (then Professor of the Social Psychology of Management at Harvard). Zaleznik's article was entitled 'Managers and Leaders – Are They Different?' Bennis's research and writing were extreme in emphasising a complete, qualitative difference between management and leadership, and he drew up a list of sharp distinctions that ended with the now familiar aphorism: 'Managers do things right, leaders do the right thing.'

While Bennis considers that managers can become leaders through learning and development, he is firm about the functional differences between the roles and the approaches involved, and the distinctions he draws echo throughout most of his writings on leadership.

The *Leaders* study

In 1979, on his return to research and teaching as Professor of Management at the University of South California, Bennis sought to unravel the lessons of his practical experience of leadership. He explored the subject through a 1985 serial study that was published as a book co-authored with Burt Nanus: *Leaders: the Strategies for Taking Charge* (1985). While Bennis has written or co-written many other books relating to leadership, these largely expand upon the ideas developed in *Leaders*.

The book aimed to identify common characteristics among ninety successful American leaders who had all, the authors considered, demonstrated 'mastery over present confusion' in their careers. They ranged from an orchestra conductor to Don Croc, the founder of McDonalds, and included a baseball player and a tightrope walker, as well as an astronaut, Neil Armstrong; 60 were chief executive officers in business, 30 were from the public sector, and all were white males apart from six black men and six women, who had to be sought out with some determination. The research was based on unstructured interviews of three to four hours and some observation. It was Bennis's second book on leadership, selling over 300,000 copies, and is still considered an important text on the subject.

In *Leaders*, Bennis and Nanus identify four common areas among the participants, and these form the core of their ideas about leadership:

- **Attention through vision.** All the leaders had an agenda, an intense vision and commitment, which drew others in. They also gave much attention to other people.

- **Meaning through communication.** All had an ability to communicate their vision and bring it to life for others, sometimes using drawings or models as well as metaphor and analogy.

- **Trust through positioning.** Through establishing the position with a set of actions to implement the vision, and staying the course, the leaders established trust.

- **The deployment of self through positive self-regard.** All knew their worth, trusted themselves and recognised their strengths as well as acknowledging but not focusing on their weaknesses. The leaders continually honed their skills. All had an agenda, an intense vision and commitment which drew others in. The leaders also gave much attention to other people.

Positive self-regard is related to 'emotional wisdom', and five key skills in emotional wisdom are given as the abilities to:

- accept others as they are
- approach things in terms of only the present
- treat others, even familiar contacts, with courteous attention
- trust others, even where the risk seems high
- do without constant approval and recognition.

One quality of these leaders that Bennis and Nanus particularly distinguished was their way of responding to failure as a learning experience. Karl Wallenda, a great tightrope aerialist, was taken as a main example. The authors illustrate his manner of putting his energies completely into his task, thinking of failure as a mistake from which he could learn, and viewing this experience (of learning based on failure) as a new beginning, rather than the end, for a project or idea.

The style of leadership discussed by Bennis and Nanus is termed 'transformative', in that it is said to have an empowering effect on others, enabling them to translate intentions into reality. A transformative leadership style is described as one that motivates through identification with the leader's vision, pulling rather than pushing others on.

Four elements of empowerment are distinguished as:

- significance – a feeling of making a difference
- competence – development and learning 'on the job'
- community – a sense of interreliance and involvement in a common cause
- enjoyment – the capacity to have fun at work because it is enjoyable and involving.

The four major characteristics of transformative leaders identified earlier are linked to strategic approaches through which a leader can:

- **Create a compelling vision.** A leader must develop and communicate an image or vision of a credible and attractive future for the organisation.

- **Translate meaning into social architecture.** Social architecture is the intangible variable that translates the buzz and confusion of organisational life into meaning. While similar to culture, social architecture is more precise in meaning, in that it can be defined, assessed and, to some extent, managed. Three styles of social architecture are distinguished as formalistic, collegial and personalistic. A leader must understand social architecture, and be able to manage or change it to mobilise the organisation to accept and support the vision.

- **Position the organisation in the outside world.** Positioning of an organisation is described as the process by which an organisation establishes a viable niche in its environment. It encompasses all that must be done to align the internal and external environments of the organisation. Trust, integrity and positioning are, it is suggested, all different faces of the ability to integrate those who act with that which must be done, so that the organisation comes together as a harmonious whole within its environment.

- **Develop organisational learning.** Good leaders are experts at learning within an organisational context, and their behaviour can help to direct and energise innovative learning within the organisation as a whole.

The end result of transformative leadership is, Bennis and Nanus consider, an empowering environment and accompanying culture, enabling employees to generate a sense of meaning in their work. Higher profits and wages, the authors suggest, inevitably accompany this sort of culture, if it is genuinely established.

At the end of the book, five myths about leadership are identified and contradicted:

- That leadership is a rare skill – it is not.

- That leaders are born – they are not.

- That leaders are charismatic – most are ordinary.

- That leadership can exist only at the 'top' – it is relevant at all levels.

- That leaders control, direct and manipulate – they do not.

Transformative leaders align the energies of others behind an attractive goal.

A later book by Bennis, *On Becoming a Leader* (1989), looks at learning to lead, developing leadership qualities and how leadership can be taught. It uses twenty-nine well-known Americans as case studies to illustrate leadership qualities.

Its main message suggests that becoming a leader involves continual learning, development and the reinvention of the self.

Bennis has since written or co-written many books and articles which expand upon and develop his ideas on leadership. His more recent works focus on the important roles of followers and groups, as well as on leadership. In *Organizing Genius* (1997), a collaborative work with Patricia Ward Biederman, Bennis almost returns to his roots in group work. The book looks at the history of seven well-known groups in action, including Walt Disney's animation studios, President Clinton's 1992 election campaign and Lockheed's 'skunk works'. Common features of these successful groups are highlighted, and the mutually interdependent relationship between great leaders and great groups is stressed.

In perspective

The importance of Bennis's work in the field of leadership is indisputable. *Forbes* magazine, for example, has called him the dean of leadership gurus. At the same time, his informal and easy-mannered style of writing and use of practical illustrations have made his books approachable, and introduced his ideas to a broad, popular audience.

The management writer Stuart Crainer emphasises Bennis's high hopes for humanity, and the consequently humane approach to leadership that accompanies these hopes. Firmly in the 'made' rather than 'born' school of leadership theory, Bennis views leadership as a skill that can be developed by ordinary people, at all levels, which centres on enabling and empowering others rather than on control and direction. He is sometimes criticised as a romantic in his approach and has himself affirmed (in *The Director*, October 1988) that he is indeed a romantic, if that term accurately describes someone who believes in possibilities and is optimistic.

Managing the bully

There is no legal definition of bullying, but the Chartered Management Institute's 2005 guidance for managers on bullying in the workplace defines it as:

Offensive, intimidating, malicious or insulting behaviour, or abuse or misuse of power, which violates the dignity of, or creates a hostile environment which undermines, humiliates, denigrates or injures, the recipient.

Bullying at work damages the health, self-esteem and morale of both those who feel they are being bullied and those who see it occurring. The human costs for people who are bullied are high in terms of long-term health problems, perceived job insecurity and effects on private life. Occasionally, people who are badly bullied at work may commit suicide.

Bullying can have serious effects for employers, possibly through legal action, but also because it can undermine productivity and performance. If undetected, one bully can increase employee stress levels and resignations, causing associated costs in absenteeism, recruitment and job training.

No single current law deals directly with how employees are treated at work, but a range of legislation can be relevant to bullying cases (including discrimination, harassment, and health and safety laws), and breach of trust or confidence may be claimed where employers fail to act on complaints about bullying or where they fail to prevent bullying, even if they did not know about it.

Bullying can be viewed in organisational or systemic terms as well as in an individual context. Bullying may be an integral part of an organisation's culture, arising from excessive hierarchical pressure to meet targets, for example, or it may simply be a problem involving two individuals, not necessarily in a hierarchical relationship, but potentially also between two peers.

This checklist provides guidance on dealing with bullying at work from a managerial perspective, at team, department or organisational level.

Action checklist

1 Create a preventative context

Make it clear by your actions and example that there is no place for bullying in your team, and establish the requirement for people to respect one another's rights and dignity. Look out for factors that can contribute to bullying attitudes, such as:

- discrimination or prejudice
- unrealistic targets or deadlines
- poor management skills
- inappropriate appraisal or performance management systems.

Consider whether existing management styles or organisational culture create an environment within which bullying tendencies may flourish. If so, seek to change this situation to reduce the risk of bullying behaviour. Establishing an ethos of mutual respect will reduce the likelihood of bullying.

2 Establish an understanding of workplace bullying

Opinions may differ about what constitutes bullying behaviour. If someone complains about bullying, the case must be investigated in a sympathetic manner and, where possible, resolved. It may be worthwhile to discuss understandings of bullying within your team. Some examples of specific behaviours that may cause or contribute to complaints of bullying are given below (many others could be added):

- aggressive behaviour involving shouting, swearing or abuse
- lack of interpersonal or communication skills, on either side
- giving people too much or too little work
- threats relating to job security
- sarcasm and ridicule
- spreading unfounded, malicious rumours
- over-stringent supervision
- physically intimidating or harassing behaviour.

3 Clarify your policy for dealing with complaints about bullying

If your organisation has a bullying policy, familiarise yourself with it. If it doesn't, develop a policy in association with your HR manager. In the UK, the ACAS Code of Practice on Discipline and Grievance sets out principles for handling disciplinary and grievance issues in the workplace.

It is often preferable (unless the situation has deteriorated too far to allow this) to follow an unofficial, off-record procedure before resorting to an official one, and to attempt to resolve the problem with the parties involved. Invoking an official course of action at an early stage could make matters worse in some cases.

4 Develop a policy

A bullying policy will help to raise awareness of the issue and communicate the message that bullying is not acceptable. It should also help prevent mishandled responses to complaints. Policies should include:

- examples of unacceptable behaviour
- a statement from senior management making bullying behaviour a disciplinary offence

- guidance on the steps complainants should take, including contact details for a trained officer for complainants who are uneasy about approaching their manager

- other possible contacts, including trade union and health and safety representatives, where relevant

- guidance for managers or others who may need to deal with complaints

- a summary of informal and formal procedures, including investigation stages and timescales

- contact details for counselling and support for all parties, if available.

5 Handling complaints

Managers need to be clear about how to proceed if an employee complains about being bullied at work. An informal approach at the start can help to avoid problems related to poor communication or lack of awareness. Important questions that need to be asked straight away include:

- What happened?

- Who was involved?

- Where did the incident take place?

- When did it take place?

- How did the complainant(s) act at the time?

- Were there any witnesses?

- Was this the first such incident, or was it part of a series of similar incidents?

- Has the complainant(s) discussed the bullying with anyone else?

- Has the complainant(s) taken any action to stop further harassment?

It is important to encourage an apology from the person(s) accused of bullying for any comments or behaviours (albeit, perhaps, unintentional or resulting from stress) that have been perceived as bullying. If the complaint is not resolved through unofficial procedures, mediation, whether with an internal trained officer or through an external independent service, can be a useful second resort, before calling upon the organisation's official grievance procedures.

If a case clearly and unambiguously involves serious bullying, however, or may relate to specific protective law (such as sexual, racial or other harassment legislation), it will be necessary to take legal advice and use the official procedures.

6 Dealing with the bully

The accused person(s) may be a manager, colleague(s) or even a subordinate(s). The context will differ for all bullying cases and is usually a crucial factor in deciding how to deal with them. Where perceived bullying has not become extreme, unofficial steps can be taken. If the complainant feels able to face and talk to the bully, it may be possible to resolve the issue yourself, or through a mediator, to the satisfaction of both parties.

Whatever course is taken, the complainant's feelings need to be a primary consideration, and the employer's concern to protect the well-being of the complainant needs to be indisputable, unless and until the case is investigated and/or resolved.

At the same time, the accused person(s) should be treated with respect, and no assumptions or judgements should be made (however well you may think you know either party). Remember that the complaint could be one of the few resulting from deliberate malice, or it could just relate to mistaken perceptions or poor communications on either side. You do not know until you investigate, so establishing any facts you can is the most important thing to do.

The accused person(s) should, ideally, be made aware of the complaint, asked about any specific matters raised and invited to give their perspective on the complaint. He or she should be moved away from the complainant, or suspended, if the complainant feels unable to work with him/her again.

If the case is found to be related to problematic but unconscious attitudes or behaviour on the part of the accused person(s), and they are willing to try to change, it may be possible to ask them to take relevant corrective training, and to monitor their work and behaviour more closely than usual for a period, rather than to suspend or dismiss them.

If consistent, deliberate and malicious bullying is found to have occurred, this misconduct will become a disciplinary issue, to be dealt with through the official procedures. For this reason, bullying and harassing behaviour should be referred to in the disciplinary policy as one of the possible reasons for dismissal.

The accused person(s) may dispute the findings, and if dismissed may take the case to a tribunal. So, by this point, you should be sure enough of the grounds to be confident in your decision.

Identifying and punishing bullies may not be sufficient. Bullying behaviour may stem from a deep need or problem. This does not excuse the behaviour, but understanding the reasons behind it can assist in trying to find positive strategies that the bully can use to meet their needs without resorting to dysfunctional strategies at the expense of others.

7 Ensure the policy is implemented

Unfortunately, but all too understandably, some managers, HR officials and even trade union representatives may have an immediate 'avoidance' response when confronted with a bullying complaint, especially if they have no training on how to respond to the situation. They could, for example:

- undermine the importance of the issue
- deny the probability of the grounds for complaint
- suggest that the complainant is being too sensitive.

While understandable, this is not helpful to any of the people concerned, or to the organisation. The complainant may accept the situation, and drop the issue, but he or she may equally decide to take it further at a later stage, if the situation worsens. Even if the complainant drops the matter completely, or decides to resign from their job, the risk of problem behaviour from the accused could remain a liability that the organisation cannot afford to carry. It is important, therefore, to implement the policy carefully, and ensure that managers are aware of their responsibility to prevent bullying, and that staff can have confidence that the policy will work, should they need to resort to it.

8 Train managers and main contact personnel

It is important to provide training to help managers and other relevant personnel to deal with the possibility of workplace bullying in an appropriate way. This will raise awareness of the issue, ensure that people understand what to do when complaints arise, and reduce the risk of mishandled complaints and legal cases.

As a manager you should avoid:

- assuming that there is no bullying in your workplace – this is unlikely to be permanently true of any organisation
- responding to complainants without demonstrating empathy and concern
- dismissing a bullying complaint, however petty or hard to believe you may judge it to be.

Redundancy: breaking the news

The basic test for redundancy is whether the employer now needs fewer employees either across the country or at a particular location. In theory, the amount of work need not have changed, but it must be capable of being carried out by fewer people.

The fact that there are to be redundancies rarely comes as a complete surprise, but telling a particular member of staff that they are to be made redundant is always a difficult task that needs to be handled with great care. This checklist offers guidance for line managers who need to inform employees that their jobs are to be made redundant. It sets out steps to follow to make the process as painless as possible for the employee concerned. The redundancy interview itself is focused upon here, rather than the process leading up to it or the statutory requirements involved in an organisation's redundancy programme.

Termination interviews are conducted on a one-to-one basis, and their purpose is to ensure that employees are given the news in a clear and objective manner, and are made aware of the reasons, the timescales involved and the redundancy package on offer.

A job is considered redundant if the employer:

- is ceasing to work in the business the employment is in
- is closing down or transferring business at a particular site
- requires fewer employees to do the type of work
- needs fewer employees to carry out work in a particular location.

Action checklist

1 Prepare yourself

All managers find it difficult to deliver bad news to their employees, and it is essential to address your own feelings towards both redundancy itself and the impact on the employee before you conduct an interview. Anticipate the likely responses and questions from the employee and consider using role-playing exercises to help you prepare.

2 Collect the information you require

To deliver the news of redundancy to an employee, it is essential to have accurate information. Make sure you are aware of and understand:

- the business reasons for the redundancy or redundancies
- the method of selecting employees for redundancy
- the details of the termination package.

Review the personal details of the employee – particularly their employment record – so you have all the facts before you meet them.

3 Plan the interview

Plan the interview carefully in terms of timing, location and what happens immediately afterwards.

- **Timing.** Although line managers may have no choice in the precise timing of delivering this news, possibly because of a decision at higher levels of management, aim to:
  - avoid holding interviews on Fridays as there may be fewer (or no) support mechanisms available to employees over the weekend
  - ensure that sufficient time is allowed for each interview (though with a clear time limit) and that there is a gap between interviews.

- **Location.** Ensure that:
  - redundancy interviews are held in a quiet, private place where you are free from interruptions, cannot be overheard and are not in the view of others
  - the employee can, if possible, leave via a different exit, to avoid embarrassment and minimise potential upset
  - the interview room is laid out appropriately; there are simple ways to avoid overt 'them and us' feelings or situations.

- **Aftermath.** It is necessary to establish what will happen to the employee as soon as he or she has been told of the redundancy. Some organisations require individuals to clear their desks (supervised by their manager or a member of the HR department) and then leave the premises immediately. Others expect the employee to work a notice period, but send them home for the remainder of the day when they are told that their job is redundant. Clarify what the organisational policy is, and whether special instructions apply to any particular positions.

- **Supporting paperwork.** Collect relevant information together to form a pack that the employee can take away and read in their own time. This should reinforce details given in the interview, and provide some information in more depth (for example, on support and advice networks to be made available to the individual).

4 Give the news

The news of redundancy is likely to be momentous for the individual concerned, so take care to give it in a clear and unambiguous manner. Do not be drawn into discussions that might unglue the redundancy programme. It is important to ensure that the individual understands the decision is final. It will help you to be clearer if you practise saying the words you are going to use out loud.

The amount of information given to an employee is critical. There is a fine line between information overload and leaving an individual with too little information. At the same time, however, everyone is different and we all react to bad news in different ways. For this reason, you need to be sensitive to how the employee is coping and decide whether the details you have to give should be brief or more extensive.

Some employees react by wanting to talk at length about their time with the organisation; others will say little. Again, being sensitive to these different reactions is important and allowing a little extra time at this stage can help curb resentment later on.

5 Provide details of what is available

Explain to the employee:

- the redundancy package (including financial settlement and other support)
- the timescales involved
- contact details of organisations that may offer help (if no outplacement service is offered).

Provide them with a copy of the information pack you have prepared and, if necessary and possible, arrange a follow-up meeting for the next week to answer further questions or clarify any problems they may have.

6 Check the employee's understanding of the situation and close the interview

Allow the employee to ask any immediate questions, and ensure that they understand the information given to them. Invite the employee to contact you again if (as often happens) further questions arise, but be firm about ending the interview to fit in with your planned timescale.

As a manager you should avoid:

- rushing the interview
- losing control in any way
- giving conflicting messages
- criticising people who are facing redundancy.

Acknowledgements

The Chartered Management Institute (CMI) would like to thank the members of our Subject Matter Experts group for their generous contribution to the development of the management checklists. This panel of over 60 members and fellows of CMI and its sister institute, the Institute of Consulting, draw on their knowledge and expertise to provide feedback on the currency, relevance and practicality of the advice given in the checklists. A full listing of the subject matter experts is available at www.managers.org.uk/policy/subject-matter-experts

This book has been made possible by the work of CMI's staff, in particular Catherine Baker, Piers Cain, Sarah Childs, Michelle Jenkins, Linda Lashbrooke, Robert Orton, Nick Parker, Karen Walsh and not least Mary Wood, the Series Editor. We would also like to thank Stephen Brough and Paul Forty of Profile Books for their support.

The management checklists are based on resources available online at www.managers.org.uk to CMI members to assist them in their work and career development, and to subscribers to the online resource portal ManagementDirect.

Index